DANGEROUS DAYS IN ELIZABETHAN ENGLAND

By the same author

Dangerous Days in the Roman Empire

Dangerous Days on the Victorian Railways

DANGEROUS DAYS IN ELIZABETHAN ENGLAND

*A history of the terrors and the torments,
the dirt, diseases and deaths
suffered by our ancestors*

Terry Deary

Weidenfeld & Nicolson
LONDON

First published in Great Britain in 2014
by Weidenfeld & Nicolson

1 3 5 7 9 10 8 6 4 2

Extract on pp. 190–1 from *Elizabeth: The Golden Age*
courtesy of Universal Studios Licensing LLC
Extract on pp. 262–3 from *Unpopular Opinions* by Dorothy L. Sayers
(Gollancz, 1946) reprinted by permission of David Higham Associates Ltd

A CIP catalogue record for this book
is available from the British Library.

HB ISBN 978 0 297 87060 9

Printed and bound by CPI Group (UK) Ltd, Croydon, CR0 4YY

Weidenfeld & Nicolson
The Orion Publishing Group Ltd
Orion House
5 Upper Saint Martin's Lane
London, WC2H 9EA
An Hachette UK Company
www.orionbooks.co.uk

The Orion Publishing Group's policy is to use papers
that are natural, renewable and recyclable products and made
from wood grown in sustainable forests. The logging and
manufacturing processes are expected to conform to the
environmental regulations of the country of origin.

For Molly Todd.
With love and thanks

CONTENTS

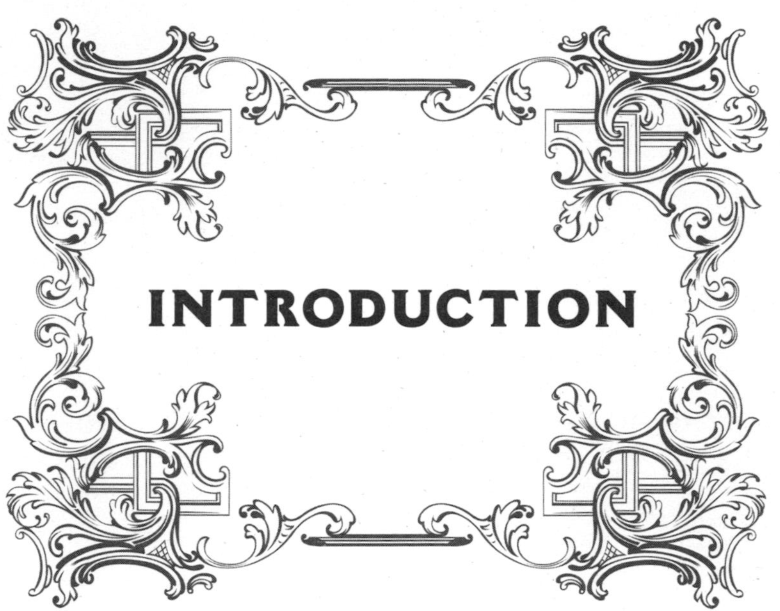

INTRODUCTION

> 'Glories, like glow-worms, afar off shine bright,
> But look'd too near have neither heat nor light.'
>
> *John Webster (c.1580–1634), English Jacobean dramatist*

The glories of the Elizabethan age shine bright as one of Queen Elizabeth I's dresses … and those dresses were so crusted with jewels they could stand up by themselves.* But what lies beneath?

Like the haunting alabaster mask of Queen Gloriana, 'look'd too near', the reality revealed a face ravaged by smallpox. Behind the painted lips there were teeth blackened by a passion for marchpane (aka marzipan). In those bold defiant eyes there is a hint of Tudor family paranoia. Queen Bess knew …

---

* A clever idea which Marks and Spencer may like to adopt as it will save a fortune on clothes hangers and rails. But please, Mr Marks and Mr Spencer, don't feel you have to write and thank me. A simple cheque in the post will do.

'Just because you're paranoid doesn't mean they aren't after you.'

Joseph Heller (1923–99), American novelist: Catch-22

Look back through the rose-tinted mists of time and there is something about the Elizabethan age that shines bright. It has the glamour of sin and bling, of beddings and beheadings, galleons and guns. We remember the school tales of a cloak in a puddle for the satin-shoed queen …

'The immaculate Sir Walter Ralegh
Had a terrible row with his valet,
Who, on seeing his cloak,
Cried, "You lousy old soak,
You've been rolling about in the alley!"'

Frank Richards (1876–1961), English writer

We remember a bold game of bowls and the woman with the heart and stomach of a king.* We remember the glories of the Globe Theatre and the scintillation of Shakespeare's powerful poetry, reminding us groundlings that we are all actors on an eternal stage. That …

'Life's but a walking shadow, a poor player that struts and frets his hour upon the stage and then is heard no more.'†

From Macbeth, *William Shakespeare (1564–1616), English playwright*

---

* We hope it wasn't her father Henry VIII's gross stomach. She was speaking metaphorically, of course, if she ever spoke those words at all.

† Oh, no. A quote from his play *Macbeth*. Will that bring a curse on me, the quoting writer … or on you the quoted-to reader? Read on and find out.

In the glow-worm light we forget that the Bard of Avon was a shrewd businessman as well as a genius writer – his admirers don't like to muddy his memory with the thought he was driven by vaulting ambition,* or that he was fuelled by the desire to escape the dunghills that scented the street-corners of Stratford.

In the glow-worm's dim dazzle of the Tudor age, we often overlook the sizzle of branding irons on tortured flesh and the cracking of joints on the rack, the hiss of living bowels as they hit the hot coals and the green glaze on the bad beef, disguised by the candle-shadow, while its smell is smothered by the stench of the cess pools – not to mention the butcher's bloodied body-odour. We forget the ordure-covered cobbles in the alleys infested by cutpurses and dummerers, by counterfeit cranks and clapperdudgeons.

We prefer to dwell on the regal ruffs – not the rufflers and roughs, the cruelty and the cockfights, the brutal bear-baiting† and the fairs filled with frauds. We may gaze adoringly at the triumph of the little ships against the obese Armada …

> 'Yarnder lumes the island, yarnder lie the ships,
> Wi' sailor lads a-dancin' heel-an'-toe.'‡
>
> *Henry Newbolt (1862–1938), English poet and historian*

---

* Oh, no. Another quote from *Macbeth*. We are really pushing our luck here. Pedants will point out that the Scottish play was written for Elizabeth's successor, James I, so has no place in a book on Elizabeth's England. To you I can only say, avaunt, you cullion, thou misshapen dick, you are a tedious fool …

† Today's reader, among whom you probably number, may be pleased to learn that sometimes the tortured bears took their revenge. A widow called Agnes Rapte was killed by Lord Bergavenny's bear when it broke loose at his house at Birling, Kent in 1563. Agnes Owen from Herefordshire was killed in her bed by a runaway bear. When a bear bit a man to death in Oxford in 1565, the bear was too valuable to be destroyed.

‡ Aharrrr, Jim lad. Don't you just love that Devon accent in yarnder pome as you warnder and parnder as you squarnder your toime.

If you want to keep your illusions of the Golden Age of elegant Elizabeth then this book is probably not for you.* If you want to hear of 'sailor lads a-dancin' heel-an'-toe' then read Henry Newbolt's Victorian rose-tinted version.

On the other hand if you want to read the truth about the Armada sailor lads, abandoned to starve on the streets, then this may be the book for you. In late August 1588, when the Armada threat had sunk, Lord High Admiral Howard wrote to Elizabeth about her sailors:

> 'There is not any of them that hath one day's victuals … many sick men are ashore here, and not one penny to relieve them. It were too pitiful to have men starve after such a service.'

And you don't do a lot of a-dancin' heel-an'-toe when you're sick with hunger.

Of course that won't surprise you, dear reader, in our own age when neglect of servicemen and women is almost as prevalent…

> 'The neglect of ex-servicemen was branded a "disgrace" yesterday as it was revealed that 20,000 are in prison or on probation in England and Wales. Figures show nearly one in ten prisoners in England are veterans.'
>
> Daily Mail, *26 September 2009*

For dreams of golden galleons go to Newbolt.

For the reality of the dangerous days in the Elizabethan world, read on.

---

* I know, it's unusual for a writer to tell a reader to stick a book back on the shelf … or burn it. But burning e-book readers is not advised as certain plastics release hydrogen cyanide when heated.

BEAUTY AND BEAST

— FAMILY FORTUNES —

> 'Ill-faced, worse bodied, shapeless everywhere;
> Vicious, ungentle, foolish, blunt, unkind.'
>
> Comedy of Errors, *William Shakespeare*

If Elizabeth defined her age then what defined Elizabeth? The answer is her family and her experiences before she came to the throne in 1558. If 'the child is father of the man' (according to William Wordsworth) then Elizabeth's experiences as a child should let us inside the head of Elizabeth the queen.

Her father, Henry VIII, looms large in her early influences. Very large. Her psychopathic father had her mother put to death when Elizabeth was two years old. That HAS to taint your views on life, don't you think?

This was part of Henry's legacy to his daughter. This horseback-breaker, this huge hill of flesh, had the one 'big idea' that changed England and the world for ever. He decided to set England free from interference from the Church in Rome.

In the world of black-and-white history he did it for selfish reasons. The typical school book says simply …

> 'Henry VIII's greatest desire was to secure an annulment to his marriage so that he could marry Anne Boleyn. The pope's inability to grant Henry VIII's request for an annulment changed the History of England forever.'
>
> *Internet History text 2014*

An eminent historian argues that …

> 'This is the moment at which England ceases to be a normal European Catholic country and goes off on this strange path that leads it to the Atlantic, to the new world, to Protestantism.'
>
> *David Starkey (1945—), British constitutional historian in Associated Press interview, 2009*

Historians like to keep things simple for us because they know we're not as clever as they are. But the truth is the Protestant movement had exploded into life with Martin Luther in Germany a full 20 years *before* Henry joined the religious revolution. He was hanging on the back bumper of the Protestant juggernaut, not driving it.

William Tyndale brought Luther's ideas to the English along with the claim that …

> 'A king's authority comes directly from God.'

How Henry VIII must have *loved* that. The tipping point of Henry's 'Reformation' in England MAY have been his wish to divorce his first wife and marry Anne Boleyn. But the Protestant revolution would have thundered into England anyway.

Why this sudden surge in Protestant rebellion against the Catholic Church? Glad you asked …

— POISONOUS POPES —

> 'All institutions are prone to corruption and to the vices of their members.'
>
> *Morris West (1916–99), Australian novelist*

Yes, ALL institutions. The Catholic Church – that barrel of righteousness – has always had its rotten apples. These days the Catholic Church scandals seem to start at the bottom.* In the Middle Ages the villainy started at the very top of the vice-ridden Vatican. The Popes were no saints. A hundred years before the Reformation it was common knowledge among the peasants and poets alike.

> 'The pope, once the wonder of the world, has fallen.
> Then came the age of clay. Could aught be worse?
> Aye, dung, and in dung sits the papal court.'
>
> *Dietrich Vrie (b. 1420), German poet*

* Please keep any smutty double entendres to yourself, if you don't mind. And speaking of apples, Anne Boleyn had a craving for apples when she was pregnant with Elizabeth. A fact which is totally irrelevant and which you should instantly forget.

Henry VIII had lived through the reigns of putrid pontiffs like …

Alexander VI (reigned 1492–1503)

- Born Rodrigo Borgia, Pope Alexander VI was famous for fattening his family's wallets at the church's expense. (Not to mention the family of his mistress.) No crime was too small for the Borgia Boys and Girls.
- His daughter, Lucrezia, became a legend as a femme fatale. When it suited the family to have her divorce husband no.1, her dad arranged it. A lover who made her pregnant ended up in the River Tiber; Pope Alexander VI said the child was his – an easy lie to swallow as he had so many children from so many mistresses.
- He was corrupt and venal, not the sort of example to set his faithful flock. Mind you his end was as spectacularly nasty as his reign. His stomach became swollen and turned to liquid, while his face became wine-coloured and his skin began to peel off. His bowels bled copiously. He was probably a poisoned pope.

Leo X (reigned 1513–21)

- He is best known for his papal bull against Martin Luther and his failure to stem the Protestant Reformation in Europe (which Henry was a little slow to join). When he became pope, Leo X allegedly said,

> 'Since God has given us the papacy, let us enjoy it.'

He then broke the papal bank, spending heavily.

- Some cardinals contrived an assassination attempt. The plotters perished from 'food poisoning'.
- If you wanted to get into heaven then Leo X would grant you an 'indulgence' … provided you could afford to pay him, he'd give you a passport through the gates of heaven. The indulgence racket was one of the sparks that kindled the Protestant fires.

Pope Clement VII (reigned 1523–34)

- Clement VII was known as a cunning diplomat. He was less bothered about the small matter of religion – even though that has to be part of his job description, doesn't it?
- Rebels besieged Rome and finally imprisoned Pope Clement VII. In one of the many colourful episodes of his life he escaped disguised as a pedlar.
- He came back to a devastated Rome in October 1528. Clement VII then kowtowed to the emperor, trying to persuade him to fight the Church's battles against the Protestant movement in Germany.

'THAT IT SHOULD COME TO THIS'

> 'Revolutions have never lightened the burden of tyranny. They have only shifted it to another shoulder.'
>
> *George Bernard Shaw (1856-1950), Irish-born British playwright*

With these travesties on the papal throne it is surprising that Henry VIII took so *long* to declare independence for the new Church of England. Of course a bonus was that Henry was able to make himself head of the Church as well as head of the State. He now ruled his people body *and* soul.

As 'reformations' go, Henry the Reformer was lukewarm as a saucer of cat's cream. The real Protestant zealots wanted to sweep away the idolatry of Catholic crosses, statues and shrines for saints, friezes and friars. Henry rather liked the theatre and glitter of the old services – he had simply wanted to take the pope's place as God's representative in his own little country.

He'd always been a good Catholic – hearing up to five masses a day (except when he needed to spend the day hunting and culling God's deer). Dismantling the monasteries was a big bonus that would put pounds in his piggy-banks. And Henry enjoyed money.

> 'Five enemies of peace live with us – avarice, ambition, envy, anger and pride; if these were to be banished, we should enjoy perpetual peace.'
>
> *Petrarch (1304–74), Italian poet*

The Reformation split the country into two camps … Protestants in power, and Catholics hiding in the candle-shadows like bad Tudor beef. Those who came out of the shadows and confronted Henry, the principled Chancellor Thomas More for example, lost their heads.*

The mutual loathing of Catholic and Protestant festered fatally through the Tudor age. By the time Henry VIII's children, Edward, Mary and Elizabeth, came to the throne it divided the country as much as the executioner's knife divided the living, writhing victims of Henry's Reformation.

When the Protestants were paramount they were pitiless … as cruel as the Catholics would be when they were top cats.

There were faults on both sides. But, whichever side you think was worse, you can be assured that religious divide led to dangerous days for everyone.

— CHEERLESS CHILD —

> 'If it would depend on popularity, Donald Duck and The Muppets would take seats in senate.'
>
> *Orson Welles (1915–85), American actor, director, writer*

Henry had been married to Catherine of Aragon, and they had a daughter Mary, which was inconvenient. And the pope refused to annul that marriage. So first Henry 'divorced' the pope, then he divorced Catherine.

Henry married Anne Boleyn, informally, when she was

* A neat new law was passed to say that anyone who denied Henry's right to be head of the Church was guilty of 'treason'. That little loophole became a convenient noose for opponents.

already pregnant. Everyone knew she was expecting a baby because she announced it (bizarrely) by telling the court she had developed 'an incredible fierce desire to eat apples'. The craving for cider inside 'er was a sign of a baby inside 'er, they knew.

Henry's second marriage wasn't a popular move among his subjects. At Anne's coronation the banners along the procession carried their initials, 'H' and 'A'. Unfortunately that meant they read 'HA! HA! HA!' … which is exactly what the crowds cried as she processed through the thronged streets.

The resulting child was doomed to be treated with suspicion by the English people. Then, as the birth approached, Anne and Henry managed to have a tiff. Over what? Over Anne's foul-mouthed rant about the king's roving eye, it seems. Eustace Chapuys, the ambassador from Savoy, wrote that Henry threatened …

> 'Anne must shut her eyes and endure, as those better than herself had done. She ought to know that he could lower her as much as he had raised her.'

Nasty. We all know what happened to Ms Boleyn, so it's not a plot spoiler to say he would 'lower her' to her knees.* That lover's quarrel, before the child was even born, was a warning light on the dashboard of the royal Rolls. She may have survived if she had given the king the son he craved.

At three o'clock on the afternoon of 7 September 1533, Anne Boleyn gave birth to a baby. The little girl had her father's red hair and long nose, and her mother's coal black eyes.

---

* If a tall person upset Elizabeth I she had a cruel little promise for them. She said, 'I will make you shorter by a head.' Was it a phrase she picked up from her dear old dad?

The prudish Chapuys gloated …

> 'The king's mistress was delivered of a girl, to the great disappointment and sorrow of the king and of the lady herself, and to the great shame and confusion of physicians, astrologers, wizards and witches, all of whom affirmed it would be a boy.'

Baby Elizabeth had been despised in the womb by the people of England. How they must have laughed, 'HA! HA! HA!' again when they heard the doleful news.

So, from the moment of her birth, Elizabeth was a 'disappointment and sorrow' to her father. In order to bed Boleyn he'd had to close down all those monasteries (with the fiscal consolation of grabbing the monks' moolah and the nuns' nickers). In 1536 he would have to face down a Catholic protest movement known as the Pilgrimage of Grace (which he managed by cheating).* And after all that, his new wife gave him a *daughter*. He was gutted … and he had a lot of gut to spill.

What a start in life for a child. If telephones had been invented she'd have been dumped in a telephone box wrapped in a rag. As she grew through childhood she must have sensed her status as a worthless human. That must have affected her character … and the history of the world.

> 'Only the unloved hate.'
>
> *Charlie Chaplin (1889–1977), English comic actor*

---

* He invited the rebel leader Robert Aske to a friendly meeting to discuss the problem. When Aske arrived he was arrested and sent to York to be hanged in chains till he died. Rebel priests were hanged from their own church steeples and fathers from trees in their own gardens. Lordly rebels had the privilege of being beheaded. They didn't do a lot of rebelling after that.

How could that happen? Anne had promised a son. The astrologers and doctors had confirmed it. Surely the stars couldn't be wrong?

A tournament to celebrate the birth of a prince was cancelled. A letter announcing the birth of a prince had been written – to save a major rewrite, an 's' was added to 'prince'.*

But the message was clear from the first breath she took. Elizabeth was 'a disappointment'.

'A LONG FAREWELL TO ALL MY GREATNESS'

'The infinitely small have an infinitely great pride.'

Voltaire (1694–1778), French writer, historian and philosopher

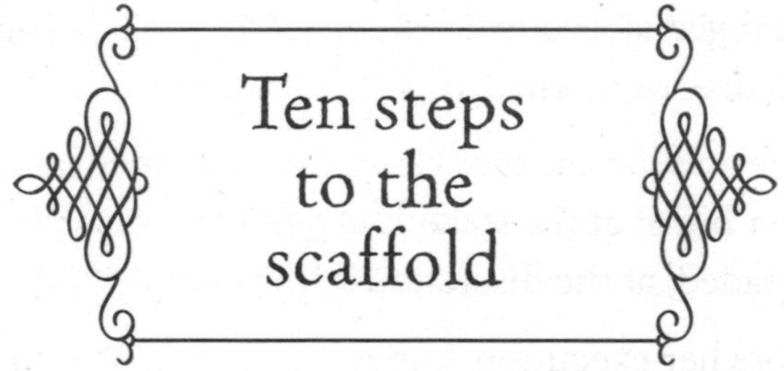

1 Two years after Princess Elizabeth was born Anne was pregnant again. In January 1536 she miscarried and Henry despaired of her ever giving him a son. He began to whinge that she had seduced him into marriage – overtones of witchcraft there.

* As Will Shakespeare would prove in later years, spelling was not a Tudor strongpoint.

2 Henry's roving eyed had roamed to Anne's maid of honour, Jane Seymour, and Anne's enemies rubbed their hands in glee. Thomas Cromwell was Henry's henchman in building a case against the queen. (He would get his own taste of the axe later.)

3 Cromwell investigated rumours about the queen's 'relationship' with her musician, Mark Smeaton. (Had he been fiddling with the queen?)

4 Musical Mark confessed … but he was being tortured at the time. (Torture us and we'd probably all confess to a little amour with Anne.) The case for the prosecution was spiced up with accusations of incest with her brother, George. For good measure she was accused of plotting to kill the king.*

5 Other men were accused of adultery and added to the charge sheet. They were found guilty and sentenced to be hanged at Tyburn, cut down while still living and then disembowelled and quartered.†

6 Anne and her brother George were sentenced to be either burnt at the stake (the punishment for incest) or beheaded, at the discretion of the king.

7 Before her execution Anne's marriage to the king was dissolved and declared invalid. One has to wonder then how she could have committed adultery if she had in fact never been married to the king.

---

* The evidence of regicide came from her flirting with Henry's valet one day. She said, 'If aught came to the king but good, you would look to have me.' And 'imagining the death of the king' was a treasonable offence. WAS she imagining his death? A technicality, but who cared. Stick it on the charge sheet.

† In fact the sentences were commuted to simply being beheaded on Tower Green. Henry was clearly an advocate of chop and change.

8 The warrant for her execution said that the king, 'moved by pity, was unwilling to commit her to the flames'. He decided to have her executed by a French swordsman.

9 The truth? The swordsman was more in keeping with Henry's self-image as an Arthurian prince. Beheading with an axe could be very messy and undignified.*

10 Henry considered every detail of his wife's death, scrutinizing plans for the scaffold in detail.

Did you know ... why Anne had to die?

When Henry started to lose interest in his queen she was furious … and indiscreet. It leaked out that she told her brother George about Henry's performance in bed. Henry had (she bitched), 'neither talent nor vigour'.

When that reached Henry's vain ears he must have been incensed. It wasn't so much a last straw as a loaded hay-wain on the camel's back.

Anne also wanted the cash from the dissolution of the monasteries to go to charity, not into Henry's coffers. Her almoner preached against Henry's chief minister, Thomas Cromwell, from church pulpits across the land.

Forget the trumped-up charges against Anne. Henry (and Cromwell) brought her down for the usual motives – sex and money.

---

* In 1540 Henry had the aged Countess of Pole, mother of a rebel, beheaded. The amateur axeman needed to chase the 70-year-old round the block then (allegedly) took 11 axe blows to finish her off. Anne's brother George was dispatched with three clumsy blows.

Anne died on 19 May 1536. The swordsman DID have some pity. He awaited her in the execution chamber and hid the sword under the straw (laid to soak up the blood). Anne was blindfolded and the executioner called out (in French) for his sword. She turned her blindfolded face to where she expected the sword to be delivered. That presented her neck nicely to the executioner who uncovered the weapon and took her head off with a single blow.

Legend has it that she died so quickly her lips were still moving after her head hit the straw. Legend doesn't tell us what she was saying. Probably, 'I don't remember this being in the prenuptial agreement?'

Cromwell had been present at the queen's beheading. He should have made notes on her dignified death because he would be executed on Tower Hill on 28 July 1540. His head was set on a spike on London Bridge. It was said of Cromwell's untidy decapitation …

> 'So paciently suffered the stroke of the axe, by a ragged Boocherly miser which very ungoodly perfourmed the Office.'
>
> *Edward Hall, contemporary chronicler*

What exactly happens when you are decapitated? Let's ask a doctor.

DANGEROUS DAYS DEATH I

BEHEADING

Your head on the block, the sword swings down, cutting quickly through the skin and underlying muscle of your neck. Momentarily slowed by the much harder neck vertebral bones and ligaments, it then accelerates onwards through the spinal cord, severing all communication with the rest of the body. That you stop breathing is not a worry, for the blade continues on through the windpipe, gullet and carotid arteries before completing its journey. As your head falls away arterial blood arcs through the air, blood pressure drops and no oxygen arrives at the brain. Most probably you die at this point, although some say you can remain conscious for a few minutes, as you watch the ground roll past.

Dr Peter Fox MB, ChB, FRCGP, DrCOG

Elizabeth was just two and a half years old when her mother faced the kindly headsman's sword.

'SO WISE SO YOUNG, THEY SAY, DO NEVER LIVE LONG'

> 'When Elizabeth smiled it was pure sunshine that everyone did choose to bask in, if they could. But anon came a storm from sudden gathering of clouds, and thunder fell in wondrous manner on all alike.'
>
> *Sir John Harington (1561–1612), courtier and Elizabeth I's godson**

Young Elizabeth – she became a motherless child with an indifferent father who was chasing the elusive butterfly of love.

Young Elizabeth had enemies round every corner. Her half-sister, Mary, was 17 years older and resented the way Anne Boleyn had taken her mother's crown. At the same time Anne's marriage had rendered Mary illegitimate. Mary had little reason to love Liz.

At Elizabeth's birth Mary was asked if she would like to pay her respects to the baby princess. She replied tartly,

> 'I know of no other princess in England except myself. The daughter of the Bolen woman is no princess at all.'

Meow.

Once Anne's marriage was annulled Elizabeth became a bastard (in the eyes of Parliament), as had her half-sister before her. Mary mellowed and gave the little non-princess Elizabeth gifts from her own pocket-money.

---

* Harington famously fell out with godmother Liz then, after years of exile from court, won his way back into her affections with his wondrous invention for the queen … a flushing toilet.

The young Elizabeth may have been part of the celebrations that heartless Henry organized for Catherine of Aragon's death in 1536.* He famously wore yellow. A gaudy expression of his sunny disposition and a display of callous contempt for a loyal woman who'd done him no harm? Perhaps. There is a theory that yellow was a colour of remembrance in her native Spain – Henry wore yellow as a sign of respect. You decide which is the more likely.

And after Anne's death (four months after Catherine of Aragon's) Henry married Jane Seymour who presented him with a son in October 1537.

We don't know when Elizabeth became aware that her mother was labelled a scheming witch and her father had had her murdered. Someone would have taken malicious pleasure in telling her, you can be sure.

> 'A cruel story runs on wheels, and every hand oils the wheels as they run.'
>
> *Ouida, pseudonym of English novelist Maria Louise Ramé (1839–1908)*†

But as the realization grew in her it must have coloured her vision of the world a bitter shade of blue.

---

* If you are looking for irony (or fate) in history then look at 29 January 1536. Queen Catherine was buried on that day. Anne Boleyn miscarried (she claimed) the son that would have saved her life, due to the shock of learning that Henry had fallen off his horse. Coincidence? Or the parting revenge shot of Catherine's ghost?

† You must have heard of her. You know, the woman who wrote *Held in Bondage* (1863). Spicy eh? Being 'proper' and Victorian it is probably comparable to *Fifty Shades of Beige*.

BRIEF TIMELINE – EARLY TUDORS

1485 Wars of the Roses end when red rose Henry Tudor beats white rose Richard III at Bosworth Field and becomes King Henry VII. He married white rose Elizabeth and everything looks rosy. It's the end of a long Plantagenet era as the rather common Tudors come to the throne.

> 'Henry the Seventh of England
> Wasn't out of the Royal top drawer,
> The only connection of which he could boast,
> He were king's nephew's brother-in-law.'*

1486 Prince Arthur is born – a Tudor heir. Even rosier.

1489 Princess Margaret born. She will become Queen of Scotland, grandmother to Mary, Queen of Scots, and give endless headaches to Henry Tudor's granddaughter, Elizabeth I. In this year Arthur (aged three) is betrothed to Catherine of Aragon (aged four) so Spain will become England's closest friend. But the best-laid plans of mice and men …

1491 Prince Henry born, second in line to the throne. A back-up in the unlikely event something happens to Arthur. And …

1502 Sod's law. Arthur dies. Catherine is passed on to younger son, Henry. Phew! Alliance with Spain saved so long as she becomes queen.

* From a monologue of Marriott Edgar – British comedian (1880–1951).

1509 Now Henry VII joins the choir invisible (whose music is the gladness of the world).* Henry VIII takes the throne … which will have to be increasingly reinforced and widened as the years go by.

1516 Princess Mary born to Hen and Cath. A girl? Curses. If at first you don't succeed, fail, fail and fail again.

1533 Catherine dumped for Anne Boleyn who gives Henry a child. Oh, dear, a girl again. She is named Elizabeth after her grandmother. She is heir, but her path to the throne has a few twists to turn yet …

DANGEROUS DAYS ON TUDOR STREETS

'Work is the curse of the drinking classes.'

Oscar Wilde (1854–1900), Irish writer and poet

'Through tattered clothes great vices do appear;
Robes and furred gowns hide all.'

King Lear, *William Shakespeare*

Henry VIII showed a cruel disregard for human life. What effect did it have on his subjects? Was he the role-model for

* As written by poet–novelist George Eliot (1819–80). I've never understood that line. If they choose to be invisible then why do they choose to let themselves be heard? Are they some sort of CD? Heard but not seen?

a cruel Tudor age? Were the days more dangerous than any other era?

As Shakespeare wisely says, there are as many villains in the wealthy classes as there are in the underclasses – the rich thieves are just more subtle than the poor ones. A pauper may kill for a crust – a millionaire will pay to have someone else do the killing … for something less life-sustaining than the pauper's crust.

Every age has had its mean streets. The Tudor age had its own brand of cut-throats and charlatans, beggars and rogues, quacksalvers and scoundrels. When Elizabeth I ruled they would hope to steal your purse – now Elizabeth II rules they will look to filch your smart-phone. Same crime really.

If you are ever offered a time-travel journey back to the 1500s then take along this guide to help you spot the cons and crooks.

The hot spots

> 'For I have sworn thee fair, and thought thee bright,
> Who art as black as hell, as dark as night.'
>
> *Sonnet 147, William Shakespeare*

London drew villains like a yellow line draws traffic wardens. The Cockney crooks had a network of information that was far more efficient than the primitive policing could cope with … i.e. you had a good chance of getting away with your misdemeanours.*

* Mind you, the downside was there would be a rope waiting for your neck if you were caught. It wasn't all caviar and champagne.

Laurence Pickering was King of the Cutpurses. In the claustrophobic world of crime, his brother-in-law was the Tyburn hangman, Bull. At first glance it may seem odd that a prince of crime was related to a paragon of the law. But we have to remember that hangman Bull's two predecessors were both convicted of theft … and hanged.*

Pickering held weekly meetings to exchange news on potential victims – 'gulls' – and the activities of the law officers. It was formal business with board meetings.

Each day they went to 'work'. It's curious that many Elizabethan villains seemed to put more effort into crime than they would have done in an honest job.

> 'Tricks and treachery are the practice of fools, that don't have brains enough to be honest.'
>
> *Benjamin Franklin (1706–90), American statesman*

If you fancy a career in crime then you may like to lurk at …

- bull- or bear-baiting rings
- theatres
- pubs and eating houses
- brothels
- gambling dens†

---

* The hanged hangmen were Cratwell in 1538 and 'Stump-leg' in 1556. What interesting executions theirs must have been. Did the victims give top tips on technique to their replacements? What were Cratwell's last words? 'Just remember, Stump-leg, take the ladder away with a sharp clockwise twist of the wrist when I tell youuuurrrrggghhhh.'

'What? Like this Mr Cratwell … Mr Cratwell? Oh.'

† In Elizabethan times there were no smart-phone apps to guide you to the prime locations, hence the need for Mr Pickering's social network.

The top tourist trap for the fleeceable foreigners and the connable country bumpkins was St Paul's Church and its 12-acre environs. Announcements to the nation were made from the cross in the centre of the churchyard; for example, in August 1588 the English people were told the Armada had been defeated. (Presumably they'd have been informed in Spanish if the result had been an away win.)

The St Paul's building wasn't as magnificent as Wren's domed masterpiece that stands there now – Elizabeth's cathedral had even suffered the indignity of having its spire demolished by a lightning strike.* If you wanted a quiet place to pray then St Paul's was not that place.

In 1561 a bishop from the sticks was shocked by what he saw at his London headquarters …

> 'The south alley for popery and money-lending, the north for selling religious pardons and favours, and the horse fair in the middle for all kinds of bargains, meetings, brawlings, murders, conspiracies, and the font for the payment of money. These were well known to all men as the beggar knows his bush.'

The criminals mingled with the lawyers, merchants and clients. Servants looking for work jostled at the 'Si quis'† door, where vacancies were posted like a Tudor Job-Centre noticeboard.

Out in the churchyard was the trendy shop that sold the fashionable new drug called tobacco. You can hear echoes of Bob Newhart's monologue as Walter Ralegh tried to sell the weed …

---

* Or maybe a thunderbolt from God, who was a Catholic but who had a few more weapons in his armoury than Guy Fawkes had?

† From the Latin *si quis*: 'if anyone'.

> 'Let me get this straight, Walt, you've bought eighty tonnes of leaves? …
>
> Then what do you do, Walt? You set fire to it! Then what do you do, Walt? You inhale the smoke, huh! You know, Walt … it seems you can stand in front of your own fireplace and have the same thing going for you!
>
> Y'see, Walt … I think you're gonna have rather a tough time selling people on sticking burning leaves in their mouths. Listen, Walt … don't call us … we'll call you …'
>
> *Bob Newhart (1929—), American stand-up comedian*

And it makes as much sense today as it did in the Elizabethan world.

Did you know … tobacco

The truth is it was the Spanish, not Walt Ralegh, who learned to smoke tobacco from native people. English sailors probably picked up the habit about 1564. Ralegh was born in 1552. Smoking tobacco in clay pipes was common in England by the time Walter Ralegh was an adult. The first Englishman to smoke tobacco certainly wasn't Walter Ralegh. It is also a myth that Walter Ralegh introduced potatoes into England.

Another two myths bite the dust.

— THE CRIMES —

> 'There is no sin except stupidity.' *Oscar Wilde*

Pamphlets were written to protect Elizabethans from being fleeced. They also laid out HOW your criminal may strike. It was almost a guidebook to becoming a crook. Of course you must NEVER put any of these tips into practice.

Nipping and foisting

> 'The robbed that smiles, steals something from the thief.'
>
> Othello, *William Shakespeare*

First spot your gull (victim) … a shambling, smelly and awed man in St Paul's would probably be from the country.

Check where he keeps his purse. It will be tied to his belt. Of course gentlemen know you are around and they keep a hand on their purse most of the time. What you need is a *copesmate* (partner) to help you distract the victim. Your partner might do this by having a *counterfeit crank* (a fit). While the gull is trying to help your copesmate, you can nip (cut) his bung (purse). You are Billy-no-mates? Cross in front of the gull and faint. Maybe add a convincing cry of, 'I say … I do feel faint.'

He will lean over to help. As he does, you grapple with him as you struggle to your feet. Again, use words to suit the action. 'Thank you, kind sir. Much obliged.'

That grappling covers the fact that you are cutting, nipping or 'foisting' ('pickpocketing') his purse. There were no pockets sewn in clothing (they hadn't been invented) and coins were carried in small leather pouches. A cutpurse might slit open the bottom of the purse, or the strings that held the purse.

Did you know ... crime times

Poaching at night would get you hanged if you were caught. Poaching by day did not.

Taking birds' eggs was also a crime. In theory it was punishable by death.

It was also a crime to travel around England without a licence, obtainable from your local bailiff. Most travellers were treated with suspicion and that's how touring actors got their reputation as rogues and vagabonds. But the restriction on travel had the practical benefit of restricting the spread of the frequent plague outbreaks.

School for scoundrels

In 1585 a London merchant called Wooton fell on hard times and came up with the answer to restoring his wealth. He set up a school for thieves.

> 'There was a school house set up to learn young boys to cut purses.* There were hung up two devices, the one was a pocket, the other was a purse. These were hung about with hawks' bells. He that could take out a counter without any noise was allowed to be a public nipper.'
>
> *William Fleetwood (Recorder of the City of London), letter to Lord Cecil*

---

* If one were a nit-picker one could quibble that the writer needed someone to learn him grammar.

By Victorian times this sort of crime-academy schoolmaster was known as a 'kidsman'. The most notorious was Ikey Solomon (1787–1850). Then along came Charles Dickens who based his timeless character, Fagin, on Ikey. Which just goes to show ...

> 'The thing that hath been, it is that which shall be;
> and that which is done is that which shall be done:
> and there is no new thing under the sun.'
>
> *Ecclesiastes 1:9*

And on the subject of 'no new thing under the sun', you'll have heard of Count Victor Lustig's scam to sell the Eiffel Tower for scrap metal in the 1920s. In Elizabethan England there were equally plausible proposals to make your fortune from ...

- dressing dog skins
- reclaiming all the submerged land of England
- making wine from raisins

As ever there were investors blinded by their own greed who swallowed the bait and the hook and were gutted.

Coney Catching

The gull was often called the 'coney' – the word literally meaning a rabbit. First find your coney's weakness.

A weakness for sex?

Offer him pornographic etchings, or a love potion that will make any woman adore him.

> 'The coney catcher can create a ring that, if a wench put it on her finger, she shall not choose but to follow you up and down the streets.'
>
> *Robert Greene (1558–92), English writer and dramatist: 'Coney-catching' pamphlet**

Not that it was difficult for a man to find a female companion – at a price – in Elizabethan London. South of the river in Southwark there were plenty of brothels (or 'stews') to choose from. They were painted white so you couldn't miss them.

They had been there hundreds of years before Henry VIII attempted to close them down. Branding with a red-hot iron was the punishment for an offender against that moral man's law.

One poet argued that closing the professional houses of ill repute just led to a burgeoning of the amateur trade.

> 'The stews in England bore a beastly sway
> Till the eighth Henry banished them away.
> And since the common whores were quite put down
> A damned crew of private whores are grown.'
>
> *John Taylor (1578–1653), the Water Poet*†

---

* Greene's warning pamphlets tell us a lot about Elizabethan villains and may be autobiographical – classic poacher turned gamekeeper. His 'Honourable Histories' are before their time. The man was so prolific he was one of the first writers able to make a living from the craft of writing. A lesson to us all. He died from 'a surfeit of pickle herring and Rhenish wine'. Another lesson.

† Taylor called himself 'The Water Poet' because he was a ferryman on the Thames, not because he wrote on water … or with water … or in the shower. He wrote over 150 publications for which he is forgotten. He is occasionally remembered for a stunt, though. He rowed 40 miles down the Thames in a boat made of paper using oars that had two fish for the blades. Take note, writers; if you're looking for fame then abandon the pen for the perch, the book for the boat.

By Mary I's time they had reopened, though laws against reckless sex were still in force. A man who attempted to sell the favours of his wife was paraded through the streets to shame him.

In Elizabeth's day prostitution was technically an offence but there were few convictions and the law didn't seem to diminish the trade. Occasionally an unlucky lady of the night would be punished by having her head shaved. A paper label was stuck to her forehead, announcing her crime, before she was paraded through the streets. A really unlucky lady would be whipped.

But there were other ways to exploit the immoral. If a man was seen with a woman who was not his wife, then he could be blackmailed. Rather more subtle was to approach the guilty man and claim, 'I am from the Court of Arches. The court that punishes adultery. I hereby charge you with immoral behaviour.'

'The scandal will ruin me,' the man may moan. 'My wife will make my life hell. Can we keep this quiet?'

'Are you trying to bribe me?'

'Yes.'

'Then that'll be twenty marks please.'

As he hands over the cash the man may mutter, 'So long as the lady's husband never hears of this!'

'Ah … so she's married too, is she?' the blackmailer leers and notes another victim. 'Thank you, sir. I presume you will not be needing a receipt. Have a nice day.'

A weakness for gambling?

> 'It had long since come to my attention that people of accomplishment rarely sat back and let things happen to them. They went out and happened to things.'
>
> *Leonardo da Vinci (1452–1519), Italian Renaissance polymath*

First you have to entice the gull to play dice … a criminal art requiring tact and perseverance, a knowledge of human weakness and experience. If art is not enough then use loaded dice to make sure the victim loses.

There were 14 different types of fraudulent dice.

- Make one side of the cube a fraction longer than the other so two numbers rarely fall. Weight the dice so high (or low) numbers invariably appear OR
- Insert a bristle on one face so the dice can't fall on that side.

Gilbert Walker's book *A Manifest Detection of Dice-Play* may help you avoid being gulled.

> 'One who makes himself a worm cannot complain if people step on him.'
>
> *Immanuel Kant (1724–1804), German philosopher*

Where could you learn the complex skills necessary to deceive the ignorant punter? The shuffles of the cards, the sleights of the dice, the patter and the flattering of the coney? There were government-subsidized courses run at the taxpayer's expense. They were called prisons.

Gambling was a sin and prohibited, of course. So much of it went on that Elizabeth and her government took a dramatic step to stop the unlawful nuisance … they made it legal.

Elizabeth's 'Groom-porter' licensed gaming houses. He had the monopoly to supply legal cards and dice. He had the right to fine cheats three shillings and four pence for each offence against fair play.

The card-sharps were thrilled. Now all the suckers would gather in a designated gambling house, all woolly and ready for fleecing. (We call them betting shops today.)

> 'The feat of losing is easily learned.'
>
> *Gilbert Walker, Elizabethan pamphlet writer:* A Manifest Detection of the Most Vyle and Detestable Use of Dice Play

You can imagine the majority of gulls would be wary of a gambler inviting them to play. But when the victim sees a drunk wander in through the tavern door, looking for a game, then he just *knows* that he can beat him. Mr Gull thinks he will become the guller. Oh, the power, the gloating, the glow of success he must feel at first.

And success washes over him like a warm stream as Mr Gull wins and wins while the drunk loses and keeps doubling his stake. You are playing 'Mumchance'. You know how it works?

- Each player names a card and places their stake on it.
- The dealer turns the cards.
- The player whose card appears first takes the pot.

But the (crooked) dealer is making sure Mr Gull has a peek at a card near the top of the pack. Easy. It's like taking rope off a baby or money for old candy.

The drunk suggests doubling the stake so he can try to re-loop his cusses … erm … recoup his losses? Of course, Mr Gull chuckles.

Soon the pot is full as a barmaid's basque. Mr Gull sees a card and calls it. The dealer turns the cards … and Mr Gull somehow loses. Every last bit of wonga gone. The drunk scoops the loot and staggers out of the door, weighed down by Mr Gull's groats, guineas and gelt.

Mr Gull has stopped chuckling. The gull has been plucked. YOU know that the drunk was all part of the con. He was known as a 'barnacle' – someone who apparently attaches himself to the game.

> 'If you're playing a poker game and you look around the table and can't tell who the sucker is, it's you.'
>
> *Paul Newman (1925–2008), American actor*

That's a modern version of the Elizabethan advice …

> 'If you play among strangers beware of him that seems simple or drunken. While you think to beguile them in their simplicity, you yourself will be most of all overtaken.'
>
> *Reginald Scot:* The Discoverie of Witchcraft *(1584)*

Two pieces of advice, 500 years apart, shows that human gullibility is an endless stream and there will always be predators ready to drink from it.

A weakness for enmity?

> 'Fire has always been and, seemingly, will always remain, the most terrible of the elements.
>
> *Harry Houdini (1874–1926), Hungarian-American illusionist and stunt performer*

Does your coney have a loathing for someone? The crafty conman will sell him a letter bomb. He can't *test* it of course. He has to trust to your honest face that it will explode when his enemy opens it. (Which it won't.)

You may prefer to flog him a magnifying glass that will focus the sun's rays and destroy anyone who walks in its path.*

* The cooperation of a sunny day is helpful here, you understand. As I am sure you will know, the 'focal length' must be positive, and is the distance at which a beam of collimated light will be focused. (Learn that

A weakness for money?

> 'A man of genius has been seldom ruined but by himself.'
>
> *Dr Samuel Johnson (1709–84), English writer*

Sell your gull the formula for making gold from goose-grease. That's what some Elizabethan gulls fell for. But not all victims were stupid people.

Even the queen's own favourite astrologer, Dr Dee, was gulled by a conman. Dee was no fool. He was a respected mathematician with advanced skills in map-making. It is probable that he used that skill to show the queen how it would be possible for English ships to reach South America and return safely.

Dr Dee also had sidelines in things like alchemy and fortune-telling. For that he needed a powerful protector like Elizabeth herself.

In 1534 a nun had been hanged because she foretold the future – she said Henry VIII would die within a month if he married Anne Boleyn. But Queen Elizabeth invited Dr Dee to read her horoscope, foretell the future and pick the best date for her coronation. He wasn't hanged, he was rewarded.

Still, astrologers were treated with either trust or contempt, exactly as they are today.

> 'They predict occurrences of the most prodigious proportions. Talk of the marvels of magic? Astrologers declare the most astonishing wonders that are about to be. These fortunate men find enough gullible people in the world to swallow their wildest announcements.'
>
> *Erasmus (1466–1536), Dutch priest and teacher*

---

by heart to impress the coney.) It also helps if your target will stand still long enough for his (or her) clothes to catch fire.

In 1569 a new law said it was a crime to speak with evil spirits. But Dr Dee chatted away with a spirit girl called Maldini and was never punished. The 'medium' was a cunning fraud called Edward Kelley.

Kelley had a stone through which he claimed he could speak to angels.* It purportedly helped him make gold from base metal with a trick that was straight out of *The Mickey Mouse Box of Magical Tricks for Infants*.† Dr Dee was fooled for ten years. When he tried to emulate Kelley's recipe for Elizabeth's benefit he failed. The queen forgave him.

Was the queen so gullible? Yes. And what of her advisors? William Cecil, Lord Burghley, was one of the shrewdest statesmen of his day and adviser to Elizabeth for most of her reign. Burghley would not be conned by the base metal to gold scam, would he? Yes.

> 'Do not let yourself be deceived: great intellects are sceptical.'
>
> *Friedrich Nietzsche (1844–1900), German philosopher*

Wrong, Herr Nietzsche. In 1588, while Dee and Kelley were in Prague, doing their tricks for Emperor Rudolf, Burghley sent for them to return to England. He asked if they would make enough gold to expand the fleet to face the Spanish Armada. Dee returned. He failed to produce the gold. Was Burghley gullible or desperate or open-minded?

> 'Do not be so open-minded that your brains fall out.'
>
> *G.K. Chesterton (1874–1936), British writer, critic*

---

* Kelley's stone also told him that the spirits wanted him and Dee to 'share' their wives. The views of the wives are not recorded.

† He used an iron rod to stir a mix of cheap materials in a heated pan and gold appeared. It wasn't an iron rod … it was a hollow tube and, as it heated, the gold melted and ran into the pan. Magic!

The clues about charlatan Kelley were there. The man always wore a tight-fitting skullcap. That disguised the fact his ears had been sliced off as a punishment for practising 'necromancy'.

He had been caught digging up corpses in a graveyard for 'ingredients'. Shakespeare would have the recipe … it wasn't all eye of newt and toe of frog. Much nastier were the human remains …

> 'Nose of Turk, and Tartar's lips;
> Finger of birth-strangled babe.'
>
> Macbeth, *William Shakespeare*

You may be pleased to know Kelley came to a nasty end. When this phoney necromancer failed to make gold for an emperor in Prague he was locked away. In his attempt to escape he fell from a tower window, broke his legs and died.

> 'My pride fell with my fortunes.'
>
> As You Like It, *William Shakespeare*

Dee died in poverty, five years after Elizabeth I, having sold his math-magical books to feed himself.

Being a conman in Elizabethan days was not without its risks.

A weakness for entertainment?

> 'My professional life has been a constant record of disillusion, and many things that seem wonderful to most men are the every-day commonplaces of my business.'
>
> *Harry Houdini*

Try conjuring. Collect money by inventing some clever trick that will draw crowds of people. If they enjoy it enough they will pay money to watch.

A juggler called Kingsfield displayed the body of 'John the Baptist' who'd had his head cut off – the head lay at the feet and it spoke.

But not all conjuring tricks were danger-free … if they *were* the public wouldn't pay to see them.

If you need to make a quick quid, pop down to your local shopping centre and try this …*

1. Take a bladder and fill it with sheep's blood.
2. Place a solid circle of wood against your stomach.
3. Place the bladder over the wood and attach it.
4. Cover the wood and blood bladder with your shirt so it looks like your beer-belly and chest.
5. Gather a crowd and announce you will stab yourself in the stomach.
6. Take a knife and invite the audience to test it for sharpness.
7. Stab the bladder of blood and fall in feigned death on the floor.
8. Have an assistant place you in a coffin.
9. The assistant can collect money for your funeral then announce you are capable of regeneration.
10. Assistant opens the coffin lid and you climb out to collect more money.

But don't try this at home.†

---

* After applying for a Health and Safety certificate from your local council … which you won't be granted when you explain what you plan to do.

† Or if you do, and you disembowel yourself, don't demand your money back for this book.

Remember you were warned that not all conjuring tricks were danger-free. A drunken conjurer outside St Paul's once forgot the wooden shield – he stabbed himself, staggered out into the churchyard … and died. No doubt there was an expression of surprise on his dead face.

Curious crimes

> 'Things do not change; we change.'
>
> *Henry David Thoreau (1817–62), American author*

The Elizabethans had some crimes that are obsolete or rare these days.

- 'Having a child out of wedlock' would earn both parties a spell in the stocks in Tudor times but earns couples family allowance benefits today.
- 'Hedge-breaking' was treated with a heavy fine in the 1500s … understandably. You couldn't have mad bulls and wild sheep set free to roam the village lanes and gore you (or fleece you). Today such criminal damage would earn you some community service – removing graffiti, picking up litter or working for a charity … 'Hedge-Breakers Anonymous', perhaps.
- 'Scolding' is no longer a punishable offence as it was in Elizabeth I's day. In 1571 a vicar's wife from Epping was punished for being 'garrulous with her neighbours'. If that were still a punishable offence then hundreds of jails would have to be constructed to accommodate all those users of social network sites.

- No one today is fined for the heinous crime of 'blocking drains'.
- Perhaps strangest was the crime of 'killing a bull and selling its meat without first baiting the bull'. The punishment for selling meat from an un-baited bull was 3 shillings and 4 pence per bull.
- 'Causing death by witchcraft' has vanished from our statute books today but would earn you a very tight noose in Tudor times.
- 'Eating meat on a Friday' is an overlooked sin these days.*
- If you were to stand up in a burger bar today and declare 'I am a reincarnation of the dead king!' you would get headlines in a red-top newspaper or two: 'Madman mimics monarch in Manchester McDonald's'.† In 1581 it got Robert Mantell dragged to the scaffold, disembowelled, beheaded and quartered.‡

---

* A law was passed early in Elizabeth's reign obliging subjects to eat fish on a Wednesday and a Saturday. The fish trade flourished, more boats were built and the number of English seamen increased. When Elizabeth turned to her sailors to defend the country against invasion they were legion … skilled and victorious. All because of a law requiring the eating of fish twice a week. Cunning.

† Suitably alliterative but, if he were claiming to be a monarch, that should logically be in Burger King. King? Monarch … oh, never mind.

‡ His near-namesake Hilary Mantel simply *wrote* about Tudor kings and queens. Her character judgements would probably have upset the Tudor monarchs and her bowels would be decorating Tower Hill. But times have changed and instead she is awarded literary prizes, which are not nearly so painful.

- Poisoning your mistress will get a female servant a life sentence today, but in 1590 it got the unfortunate wench burned at the stake.
- 'Maliciously letting out of ponds' … don't do it.
- 'Brawling in court' will still earn you a punishment … probably a spell in the cells. In Elizabeth's more logical age you'd have had the offending fists cut off, which would leave you not so pleased as Punch.

— THE PUNISHMENTS —

Every silver lining has a cloud. And the downside of exploiting your fellow man was the punishment if you were caught.

> 'Rogues and vagabonds are often stocked and whipped; scolds are ducked upon cucking-stools in the water … Thieves, if they have stolen nothing else but oxen, sheep, money, or such like, which be no open robberies, as by the highway side, or assailing of any man's house in the night, without putting him in fear of his life, or breaking up his walls or doors, are burned in the left hand, upon the brawn of the thumb, with a hot iron, so that, if they be apprehended again, that mark betrayeth them to have been convicted before, whereby they are sure at that time to have no mercy.'
>
> *William Harrison:* Description of Elizabethan England *(published 1577–78)*

You could also suffer …

- being burned through the gristle of the ear
- being whipped on the back till you bled
- hands cut off*
- ears sliced off
- hanging … of course

Holy places were not exempt from the perils of punishings. If the displays of booksellers at St Paul's didn't amuse you then there were other treats on offer. From time to time gallows would be erected at the west door of the cathedral. In January 1560 this accommodated two convicted men, guilty of crimes committed within the confines of the churchyard. The corpses hung there all day before they were stripped and the bodies thrown into a common grave. (This probably gave the sinners who infested the churchyard a pause for thought … but only a pause.)

> 'Rarely does a law day pass in London without some twenty to thirty persons, men and women, being hanged at Tyburn.'†
>
> *Thomas Platter the Younger (1574–1628), Swiss doctor and traveller:* Travels in England

---

* A punishment handed out to a couple of attempted poisoners in 1559. They lost their ears too.

† An exaggeration. But not a vast one. On some days the surgeons were allowed to take the corpses for dissection and experiment. As criminals were treated more leniently over the next 200 years the supply of good anatomy research material dried up. Supply and demand meant the trade of body-snatching flourished. A grave offence.

Prisoners would be taken to the Tyburn gallows – a triangle of beams – on a cart. The nooses from the beams would be slipped around their necks, a leather hood placed over their heads and the cart driven away, leaving them to dangle and strangle. Tyburn offered execution on an industrial scale – 24 could hang at any one time.

Tyburn did not have a monopoly on hangings. Gallows popped up in various locations around the city of Good Queen Bess.* Especially juicy murders would earn the killer an execution close to the spot where he or she committed the crime. Perhaps that assuaged the grief of the victim's relatives – or satisfied the lingering spirit of the victim.

Pirates were treated to a hanging at the low-water mark at Wapping Dock where visiting ships could see the sea-robbers cool their feet in the Thames.

The pillory held the head and hands in a frame while the criminal was forced to stand for hours. It was the sort of funfair attraction you see in heritage sites today, but no one threw wet sponges at the laughing victim. Those who felt faint after a spell in the pillory could strangle themselves if their legs failed to support them.

In 1561 a man started a fight in St Paul's churchyard and the pillory was his punishment. His ears were nailed to the frame and his release was effected by the direct expedient of slicing them off. Tradesmen who sold bad food would have their rotten produce hung under their noses. A paper crown might be placed on the head, with a note naming the crime for passing strangers.

---

* London wasn't as spectacular as the Coliseum as a killing ground, but it was still a chilling piece of criminal control. Crime continued, so it looks like an argument against the 'Bring back hanging' brigade. Thousands of instances of capital punishment in the capital city didn't appear to work as a deterrent in the Elizabethan world.

In 1563 a woman was pilloried for eating meat during Lent. That seems harsh. Three months later a schoolmaster was pilloried for beating a boy with a belt buckle till the skin was torn off the boy's back. That seems lenient.*

The stocks – having the feet fastened – was usually the prelude to a whipping. The French refined this in a torturous twist. They threw a bucket of cold salt water over the victim's bare feet then allowed a salt-loving goat to lick the soles of the criminal. The English racks and red-hot pincers were not so cruel. The Marquis de Sade was French. Says it all.

Royal revenge

In 1580 there were negotiations to marry Elizabeth off to a French prince. Of all Elizabeth's suitors, Francis, the French Duke of Alençon, conducted the final and most determined bid for the Queen of England. The queen was approaching 50.†

Many English strongly opposed such a marriage; prominent Puritan John Stubbs openly published a book titled *The Discovery of a Gaping Gulf whereunto England is like to be swallowed by another French Marriage.*‡ With no training in a Swiss ladies' finishing school he said tactlessly …

---

* Today he would be sacked and exposed in the *Daily Mail* – the 21st-century equivalent of the pillory. A year later the teacher would be quietly reappointed by the Department for Education as a schools inspector in the Ofstapo department.

† As a princess, Elizabeth was linked to 10 suitors. When she became queen there were a further 15. She was as popular as an ice-cream on a warm day … but stayed just as cool.

‡ Catchy title, no? If that were available on e-books at 99p it would surely hit the bestseller charts.

> 'It is a contrary coupling, an immoral union, an uneven yoking of the clean ox to the unclean ass, a thing forbidden in the law as laid down by St Paul. It would draw the wrath of God on England and leave the English pressed down with the heavy loins of a worse people and beaten as with scorpions by a more vile nation.'

Strong stuff. Elizabeth was not amused … even if she was the clean ox. She ordered that the right hands of those responsible be cut off – the hands that had offended her. Stubbs (whose hand would soon be a stub) came up with a pun that would get him booed off the Glasgow Empire. As his hand was hacked, he proclaimed …

> 'Pray for me now my calamity is at hand.'

Laugh and the world laughs with you. He removed his hat with his left hand (obviously) and cried 'God save the queen,' before fainting. As you would.

His co-conspirator, the publisher William Page, held up his bleeding stump, and said: 'I left there a true Englishman's hand' … which doesn't even qualify as a witty pun as he 'left' there his 'right' hand.

Elizabeth's publicity machine got it wrong on this occasion.

> 'The multitude standing around was altogether silent, either out of horror at this new punishment or out of pity towards the man, or else out of hatred of the marriage.'

And the most punning irony of all? Elizabeth was offering her 'hand' in marriage.

Halifax law

> 'From Hell, Hull, and Halifax, Good Lord, deliver us!'
>
> The Beggar's Litany, *John Taylor, the Water Poet*

Praying for deliverance from Hell is obvious. But Hull and Halifax?

Hull had a harsh policy of whipping beggars.

Halifax? If the 'three-strikes and you hang' rule was a harsh London law then the Cockney villains must have been pleased that they didn't live in Halifax in Elizabeth's reign. A 1577 law confirmed …

> 'At Halifax, if a theft be valued by four constables to amount to the sum of thirteen and a half pence, he is forthwith beheaded.'

The beheading was carried out at the Halifax Gibbet – an embryonic guillotine.*

For stealing something worth a shilling you would lose your head.†

Except … there was a curious custom. The axe dropped when a wooden peg was pulled, and if you could get your head out before the axe hit your neck you were free to leave Halifax – so long as you never returned.

---

* There is a replica in Gibbet Lane, Halifax, today. Go and see it. Quickly. Chop-chop.

† Juries often undervalued the stolen property to avoid passing the death sentence.

On 29 January 1623 John Lacy managed this feat and escaped. But after seven years, the Running Man (as he was nicknamed) foolishly believed that he would be allowed back. There was no such provision in the Halifax law. As soon as he returned he was put back under the blade … and this time he didn't make the great escape. Lacy lopped at last.

Play off final

Richard Vennor sold tickets for plays that were never performed and pocketed all the money. It was known as cozening. But, in the end, he was caught and thrown in prison.

At first Vennor used his money to buy a private cell, good food and wine from the jailer. But, when the money ran out, he was thrown in 'the Hole' to sleep on bare boards with 50 other men, women and children. The cold in winter or the disease in summer or the bad food killed anyone who stayed too long. A poet said of the Hole …

> 'In the Hole you are buried before you are dead.'
>
> *Thomas Dekker (1572–1632), Elizabethan poet and dramatist*

Richard Vennor died. Cozening can be bad for your health.

MURDER AND MAYHEM

> 'It is foolish to tear one's hair in grief, as though sorrow would be lessened by baldness.'
>
> *Cicero (106–43 BC), Roman orator*

As a baby Elizabeth had been packed off to Hatfield or Hunsdon or Hertford, Rickmansworth or Richmond … houses around London. Half-forgotten, but at least safe from the plagues that ravaged the city.

In 1537 Henry VIII's son and heir was born to his third wife, Jane Seymour. Elizabeth, aged four, was invited to carry the baptismal robe when the child was christened.

A month later and the royal family was back in church for the funeral of Jane Seymour – childbirth was a dangerous thing, even for a queen.*

The princesses Mary and Elizabeth slipped down the

---

* Pub-quiz enthusiasts may care to note that Jane Seymour was the only one of Henry's six wives to be buried with the title of 'queen'.

league table of heirs. They may yet have had their uses as marriage prospects for political alliances, but Henry had debased their value by having them declared bastards. So, generally, they were a drain on the exchequer.

They often passed the time playing cards and Elizabeth began to display the temperamental side of her personality. No one dared to beat her at cards. If she lost she sulked. It was easier (albeit more expensive) to let the spoilt child win. While most Tudor workers were lucky to earn two or three pounds a year, one of Elizabeth's courtiers, Lord North, lost ten pounds every week playing cards with her. He was almost ruined.

— ANOTHER DAY, ANOTHER WIFE —

> 'Present: (noun). That part of eternity dividing the domain of disappointment from the realm of hope.'
>
> *Ambrose Bierce (1842–1914), American author & satirist:* The Devil's Dictionary

Elizabeth, as third in the line of succession, was able to grow up in relative obscurity and calm. Big sister Mary mellowed and became a surrogate mother.*

Henry was off on the marriage merry-go-round again when he married (briefly) Anne of Cleves. He courted her on the strength of a painted portrait. She landed on 27 December 1539 and they married on Twelfth Night 1540. But Anne of Cleves was a Christmas toy that disappointed as

* Some writers would say that Mary became head of the household because Anne Boleyn was in no position to head anything. But that would be really too tasteless, wouldn't it?

soon as it was unwrapped then discarded before the batteries had run out. She wasn't pretty enough for him.

Cowardly Henry hadn't the courage to upset his allies by rejecting her outright. So he married Anne, then seethed against his ministers for dropping him in this mess. He claimed, pitifully, he was marrying 'to satisfy the world and my realm'.

He blamed advisor Thomas Cromwell. But he couldn't bring himself to consummate the marriage … not even for 'the world and his realm'. Or maybe he simply wasn't up to it … and Viagra hadn't yet been invented.

Meanwhile, Anne's maid of honour, Catherine Howard, had caught the king's eye. She was a cousin to Anne Boleyn. Nothing like keeping it in the family. Or maybe Henry was haunted by his murderous act and wanted a Boleyn girl, 1540 model.

Certainly he was not a man who learned from his mistakes. He prepared to jump from the dull frying pan into the sparkling fire.

> 'A particularly beautiful woman is a source of terror. As a rule, a beautiful woman is a terrible disappointment.'
>
> *Carl Jung (1875–1961), Swiss psychiatrist and psychotherapist*

Anne of Cleves was divorced … and none-too emotionally scarred by the event.* She retired on a pension in England and joined the royal satellite family, being an especial friend of Princess Mary. (They had both had their lives transformed by a Henrician divorce.)

---

* Let's face it, as traumas go, being divorced by Henry is better than being beheaded on his orders.

On 28 July 1540 Henry married Catherine Howard. On the same day Thomas Cromwell was beheaded. Someone had to suffer for the cock-up over Anne of Cleves … or maybe, in the circumstances, 'cock-up' is the wrong metaphor?

Teen queen Catherine made a fuss of little Elizabeth. They sat opposite one another at the royal banqueting table. Tragic for both. When Catherine suffered the same fate as her cousin Anne Boleyn, the impact on Elizabeth's psyche must have been even more traumatic than the death of her mother (when she had been too young to take it in).

> 'Crime butchers innocence to secure a throne, and innocence struggles with all its might against the attempts of crime.'
>
> *Maximilien de Robespierre (1758–94), French lawyer and politician*

If anything it was Henry VIII who had been innocent and naïve. He believed the flirtatious and vibrant young queen was untouched by men. It was reported that she had lovers before her marriage to the king. Then rumour said she had adulterous affairs *after* she married the gross older man with ulcerated legs. The man of whom Cousin Anne said had 'neither talent nor vigour' in the royal rumpy department.

Henry's vanity refused to believe Catherine's accusers for a while – how could *any* woman find a better love?

> 'The king has changed his love for the queen into hatred, and taken such grief at being deceived that of late it was thought he had gone mad, for he called for a sword to slay the woman he had loved so much.'
>
> *French ambassador (1541)*

As Henry accepted the truth the rage turned to self-pity. What had he done to deserve such 'ill-conditioned wives'?*

Soon the misery turned to vicious cruelty. She had to die. When Catherine heard of her impending fate she raced through the corridors of Hampton Court Palace screaming to Henry for mercy. His door was locked, his ears were closed and his heart was hardened.†

When Dr Hawley Harvey Crippen famously killed his unfaithful wife in 1910 he was executed. When Henry VIII had his unfaithful wife murdered he was excused.

> 'Everyone knows that there is one law for the rich and another for the poor. But no one accepts the implications of this, everyone takes it for granted that the law, such as it is, will be respected, and feels a sense of outrage when it is not.'
>
> *George Orwell (1903–50), English novelist*

Wrong, Mr Orwell. Henry VIII seems to have escaped the outrage. 'Bluff King Hal' remains in folk-memory as a noble figure. His excesses were tolerated because, after all, he was God's chosen representative on Earth.

Perhaps Jonathan Swift was more accurate in his view of the law …

> 'Laws are like cobwebs, which may catch small flies, but let wasps and hornets break through.'
>
> *Jonathan Swift (1667–1745), Anglo-Irish satirist*

---

* Answers on a very long scroll of parchment, please, when you have a few spare months.

† Her screaming ghost can be seen at the palace, it is said.

Catherine Howard was beheaded and buried alongside Cousin Anne on 13 February 1542. Her little protégée Elizabeth was eight years old and must have been painfully aware of the empty chair at the royal table.

Later that year a baby was born in Scotland. She was christened Mary and within six days that baby had become Mary, Queen of Scots.* She would never get to meet Cousin Elizabeth … but their lifelines were to be as conjoined as a pair of Sumo wrestlers.

— SEEDY SEYMOUR —

> 'The change of place did not vex me so much, dearest sister, as your going from me.'
>
> *Prince Edward, letter to Princess Elizabeth*

Eighteen months after the Howard horror Elizabeth was given her fourth stepmother, Catherine Parr. A mature woman of 31, twice widowed before she married Henry … and it would be third time unlucky for Henry.

Elizabeth and heir Edward shared their schoolroom until 1546. The old, rotting, warthog king lumbered towards his final year. And when he was too ill to lumber he was carried in a chair, bad-tempered and raging from pain and fever. In January 1547 he died.

---

* King James V of Scotland was another victim of Henry VIII. When matrimony went wrong, Henry turned to war against James's Scots to vent his anger. English armies defeated them at the Battle of Solway Moss. That defeat seemed to occasion a nervous collapse of James V and he died, leaving new-born Mary to become Queen of Scots. If Henry VIII DID bring about James V's death then it is ironic that Henry's daughter would bring about the death of James's daughter.

Young Edward was king. Elizabeth and Edward wept on one another's shoulders when the news was broken to them. Elizabeth had climbed the ladder to be second in line to the throne.

Edward's uncles, Thomas and Edward Seymour, would tussle for control of the young king's power. Henry had not nominated a 'regent' but left a council in charge until Edward was old enough to rule for himself. That failure to name a single regent left a vacuum that the Seymours raced to fill.

Edward Seymour assumed the reins. Thomas Seymour seethed. The unscrupulous and vain man thought a pathway to the top lay in marrying either Mary or Elizabeth. To hedge his bets, he chanced his arm with both.

The council blocked his scheme so he turned his attentions to an old flame … the now 34-year-old ex-queen, Catherine Parr. He knew that he was the love of her life and sure enough, she accepted. It would be a fair guess to say she didn't know he'd been eyeing up her stepdaughters.

> 'Truly as God is God my mind was fully bent to marry you before any man I knew. God is a marvellous man.'
>
> *Catherine Parr (1512–48), letter to Thomas Seymour*

To which our reaction is either, 'Awwww, bless.' Or 'What a mug!'

They were married in secret. We don't know what Elizabeth thought, but it seems Mary was furious at the haste with which her father had been forgotten. Three or four months do not a period of mourning make, according to the princess.

> 'The scarcely cold body of the king has been shamefully dishonoured.'
>
> *Mary Tudor – reported by Gregorio Leti, Elizabeth's biographer*

But the new King Edward blessed the marriage. Maybe he didn't know about Thomas Seymour's distasteful peccadilloes.* Elizabeth was 13 years old and living with Catherine Parr and her secret husband when he would …

- Arrive in Princess Elizabeth's bedroom before she was out of bed or when she was getting dressed.
- Draw the curtains around her bed and pretend to lunge at her while she tried to evade him.
- Give her playful slaps on the back or on the buttocks.
- Attempt to kiss her (though she was saved by the presence of her maid, Kat Ashley).
- Tickle Elizabeth in her bed and shred her dress (while Catherine Parr held her down).

A year later and Catherine Parr was pregnant with Thomas's child. She caught Thomas and Elizabeth (now 14 years old) in some sort of embrace and her fury was explosive. Elizabeth was moved out of the Seymour household.

If Thomas had been 'grooming' the princess then it was a dangerous game. It seems Elizabeth wasn't entirely innocent and the man's attentions weren't entirely unwelcome. Elizabeth wrote to stepmother Catherine with 'sorrow' and said she was grateful that Catherine offered to report any gossip arising from the 'embrace' incident.

> 'You said you would warn me of all evils you would hear of me.'
>
> *Elizabeth, letter to Catherine Parr*

* A euphemism. After all we can't call a lord of the land a dirty old man … or a paedophile, can we?

There would be no evil reports without some substance – no smoke without fire.

Catherine had acted quickly to put a stop to it. But who was 'saved' by her intervention – Elizabeth or Thomas Seymour?

> 'Innocence does not find near so much protection as guilt.'
>
> *François de La Rochefoucauld (1613–80), French author*

Sadly, not long after this Catherine Parr would abandon Elizabeth for good. After giving birth to a daughter she died.

Elizabeth was about to embark upon the most dangerous decade of her life with no mother-figure to guide her. She had seen off a mother and three stepmothers.

> 'To lose one parent may be regarded as a misfortune; to lose both looks like carelessness.'
>
> *Lady Bracknell in* The Importance of Being Earnest, *Oscar Wilde*

BRIEF TIMELINE – ELIZABETH'S EARLY YEARS

1540 Thin, pockmarked Anne of Cleves doesn't please Henry VIII. He divorces her quickly and has Thomas Cromwell, the man he blames for the debacle, beheaded. With a blunt axe.

1542 Now it's wife no. 5's turn for the axe. Catherine Howard is executed for adultery. The Scots in turmoil as James V dies suddenly and leaves the throne in the hands of Mary, Queen of Scots, aged just six days. Henry's niece is probably higher up the ladder to the English throne than the illegitimate Elizabeth. There may be trouble ahead …

1543 Now Henry marries Catherine Parr. Her Protestant conservative enemies try to have her prosecuted for her radical Protestant beliefs.* As Elizabeth's last stepmother she will influence the princess's thinking.

1546 Henry is slipping away and the Protestant conservatives are defeated in their plans to control Edward VI's rule when he succeeds. More executions. The family of Henry's favourite wife, the Seymours, are in the ascendancy when …

1547 … Henry VIII turns up his toes. The radical Protestants control the kingdom. Catherine Parr marries one of them – the devious Thomas Seymour.

1548 As the English invade Scotland young Mary, Queen of Scots, flees to France where she will eventually marry the French king.

1549 Rebellions to the west, rebellions to the east. Poor harvests, stagflation, new prayer book, fences round common pasture … you name it and rebels will rise … and be crushed quite ruthlessly. But chief crusher, Protector Lord Somerset, will soon end up in the Tower of London.

---

* An arrest warrant was drawn up for Catherine Parr accusing her of heresy. She went to Henry and more or less said, 'I only argue religion with you to take your mind off your illness. I'm not really a heretic, my love … let me put new bandages on your suppurating, stinking, oozing, festering wound?' She escaped the stake and survived the king. Clever lady.

— TUDOR MURDER —

> 'It is forbidden to kill; therefore all murderers are punished unless they kill in large numbers and to the sound of trumpets.' *Voltaire*

The first crime ever, according to the Bible, was murder.*

And murder was as grimly fascinating in the Elizabethan world as it has ever been. Playwrights entertained crowds with terrible tales of every sort of homicide imaginable. Hamlet's father was killed with poison poured into his ear … a plot device even Agatha Christie would have been proud of. By the end of the play *Hamlet* there are at least ten corpses to count and a rich array of murder methods.

But there were violent ends to lives in the real world too. Not just the murderous muggings on the mean streets and unlit alleys. Even the top people were topped. And one person who seemed to attract the Grim Reaper like a magnet attracted his scythe, was Elizabeth's cousin … Mary, Queen of Scots.

Common killing

> 'Let's kill him boldly, but not wrathfully;
> Let's carve him as a dish fit for the gods,
> Not hew him as a carcass fit for hounds.'
>
> Julius Caesar, *William Shakespeare*

---

* All right, Eve had disobeyed God by eating an apple from the forbidden tree, but that particular crime is no longer on the statute books. The first 'crime' for which you'd be locked away today was Cain's murder of Abel. The story of Cain and Abel was probably the world's first crime story.

The average life span of a person in Tudor times is generally reckoned to be around 40. But that figure is distorted by high infant mortality rates (25 per cent of children died before their first birthday, and 50 per cent before their tenth). So if you were a man, aged 21, you could expect to live to around 67.

It's a myth that life was 'cheap'. Murder was as heinous a crime then as now. But there were differences.

A wife who killed her husband did not commit murder – she committed the far worse crime of 'petty treason'. The punishment wasn't then a quick and painless hanging but being burned at the stake.

A foreign visitor to England summed up the punishment system in a book in 1578 …

> 'If a woman poison her husband, she is to be burned alive for petty treason; if a servant kill his master he is also to be executed for petty treason; he that poisons a man is to be boiled to death in water or lead, even if his victim does not die.* In cases of murder all those who help the murderer are to suffer the pains of death by hanging. Many crimes are punished by the cutting off of one or both ears. Rogues are burned through the ears and sheep-stealers punished by the loss of their hands.'

And there were similarities to today's fascination with lawlessness; the voyeuristic public wanted all the grim and gruesome details of the crime and its punishment. There

* Boiling alive was a law introduced by Henry VIII and repealed after his death. But the few who suffered it were not dropped in boiling water to die a quick lobster death. They were placed in a cauldron of cold water that was slowly heated to boiling. Prolonged agony.

were no red-top newspapers to satisfy their lascivious lust for gore, but pamphleteers met the need.

The Elizabethan public enjoyed witnessing executions too. A pamphlet described the immense size of the audience, and the social cross-section, when Ann Saunders was executed (see her crime below). The Earls of Derby and Bedford were there and …

> '… so great a number of people as the like have not been seen there together in any man's remembrance. People thronged the routes from Newgate to Smithfield and watched from nearby rooftops, steeples and houses whose windows and walls were in many places beaten down to look out.'
>
> *Pamphlet 1573*

The public nature of the executions was meant as a warning to deter criminals. The fact that so many cutpurses roamed through the crowds may be a little clue that the medicine wasn't working?

So what notorious crimes *did* Elizabethan families discuss around the breakfast table? What tales of terror were told to put them off their porridge?

Murder most foul

1 The slaughter of the innocent

> 'The croaking raven doth bellow for revenge.'
>
> Hamlet, *William Shakespeare*

Ten robbers burst into an Essex house and stabbed the parents of young Elizabeth and Anthony James.

The children were carried off to a house near Hatfield where Anthony was murdered. Elizabeth was handed over to the gang's moll, Annis Dell. She hadn't (quite) the heart to slay the little innocent … so she cut out the child's tongue and abandoned her to die in a forest.* Kind locals rescued and cared for the girl. Four years later Elizabeth stumbled on the house of Annis and, using signs, had the woman arrested. The court required spoken testimony and somehow the tongueless girl found the voice to describe her ordeal. A miracle. (The Elizabethans loved that.) Annis was duly hanged. The robbers seem to have escaped. It would have been sweet revenge for Elizabeth … had she had the power to taste sweetness, of course.

* So far so Grimm's fairy tale isn't it?

2 The eternal triangle, 1573

> 'There is no greater glory than love, nor any greater punishment than jealousy.'
>
> *Lope de Vega (1562–1635), Spanish playwright and poet*

It's a story that will happen today somewhere in the world. George Browne was in love with Ann Saunders … but she was married to George Saunders, a rich London merchant-tailor. So Browne waited for Saunders at Shooter's Hill near London and murdered him. He was arrested. A few days after the murder Ann gave birth to her fourth child. Was the timing significant? Was Browne the father of the baby? The law thought so and Ann was arrested too. Had she encouraged lover Browne to murder her husband? She denied it … but was sentenced to hang anyway.* She confessed before they executed her.

3 Bewitched and bothered, 1589

> 'Witchcraft is one of the most baseless, absurd, disgusting and silly of all the humbugs.'†
>
> *P.T. Barnum (1810–91), American showman*

Alice Samuel (1513–93) was the wife of John Samuel of Huntingdonshire. In 1589, ten-year-old Jane Throckmorton

---

* Yes, husband murder was supposed to be punished by burning at the stake. Maybe being simply an accessory earned her a little leniency. She still ended up dead of course.

† Wise words from one of the world's leading exponents of humbug. He made a mint from humbug.

suffered an epileptic attack and accused Alice of using witchcraft against her. Soon Jane's four sisters, aged from nine to fifteen, and seven of the family's servants, began to imitate Jane's symptoms – probably to earn a share of the attention she was getting. Alice was forced to move in with the family as a servant.

In 1590, Lady Cromwell had a spat with Alice and the servant uttered the fatal words, 'I never did you any harm … yet.' Soon after, Lady Cromwell fell ill and died in July of 1592. The local pastor, Dr Dorrington, accused Alice of witchcraft and she was tortured into confessing. She even admitted to having three familiars – chickens named Pluck, Catch and White. Alice, her husband and daughter were all found guilty of murder by witchcraft and hanged.

4 Sleeping dogs die, 1592

> 'If you poison us do we not die? And if you wrong us, shall we not revenge?'
>
> *Shylock in* Merchant of Venice, *William Shakespeare*

A similar fate awaited John Brewen. He was a hard-drinking, wife-beating goldsmith. His punch-bag, Anne, had affairs with various men to escape the misery. Brewen had wooed Anne with jewels into wedding him, but she had always preferred his fellow goldsmith, John Parker. Sneaky Brewen blackmailed her into marriage – he said Anne had stolen the jewels from him – much to the rage of Parker. Parker urged Anne to kill Brewen but she was reluctant. The tipping point came when Brewen poisoned her beloved dog. Her revenge was to poison Brewen – with Parker's help. Revenge for caninicide was not taken into consideration as a mitigating circumstance. Anne and Parker hanged at Smithfield.

5 Sod's law, 1579

> 'If people are good only because they fear punishment, and hope for reward, then we are a sorry lot indeed.'
>
> *Albert Einstein (1879–1955), German-born physicist*

Thomas Appletree. Poor sod. He was having a laugh. He was with a group of friends who were rowing down the Thames when he loosed a few pistol shots to show off and 'test' his new gun. One shot injured a man who was rowing a barge. Stupid … but forgivable? No. It was the queen's barge. Oooops.

The queen was on board with the French ambassador at the time. Double Oooops. There were reports of Catholic assassination plots against Elizabeth, who was negotiating a French marriage at the time. Triple Oooops. So the laddish lark put a noose around Appletree's neck. In a theatrical touch, his gallows were built by the side of the river where the offence occurred. Appletree climbed the scaffold with the rope around his neck. As he grovelled for forgiveness the queen's chamberlain stood alongside him and explained to the crowds why Appletree deserved to be chopped. Then he concluded …

> 'And now, if it please you, you may with marvel hear the message I come with*… I bring mercy to this man the most gracious pardon of our most dear sovereign, who with merciful eye vouchsafes to rob him from the gallows.'
>
> *Sir Christopher Hatton (1540–91), favourite of Elizabeth and Lord Chancellor of England*

* Picture, if you will, the drum roll and dramatic pause at this point.

The crowd cheered, 'God save the queen'. Which is, of course, exactly what the 'merciful-eyed' lady wanted. She was her own best spin doctor.*

6 Dramatic death

> 'History is, indeed, little more than the register of the crimes, follies, and misfortunes of mankind.'
>
> *Edward Gibbon (1737–94), British historian, writer*

Thomas Arden of Faversham was a rich man, trading on the miseries of the monasteries. He was one who profited from Henry VIII's reformation. But money can't buy you love ... a sentiment echoed by Messrs Lennon and McCartney almost 500 years later. Tom's wife Alice fancied a bit of rough, a brother of her maid called Mosby. Alice and Mosby botched several attempts on Tom's life, then they hired two soldiers to do the job. Amazingly it took the pair of privates a few bungles before they finally killed their prey in his home on Valentine's Day 1551.† They dragged the body through a snowstorm and dumped it in a field. But then it stopped snowing. Rotten luck. The local Sherlocks were able to follow the footprints back to Arden's house, where they caught the killers red-handed ... literally. Alice was burned alive. The story was perpetuated in the play *Arden of Faversham* and a young Shakespeare may have had a hand in the writing.

* Around a hundred royal pardons were issued each year.

† There was a Valentine's Fair in Faversham and the killers calculated suspicion would fall on the itinerants who flocked in. Smart thinking.

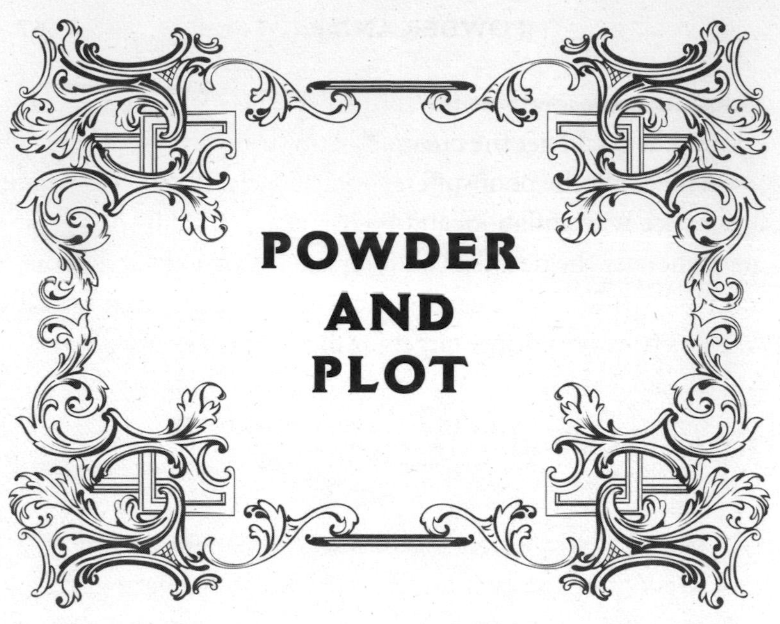

POWDER AND PLOT

— RUTHLESS REBELLION 1549 —

Elizabeth must have lived and worried through all the Tudor tensions and seemed to believe that repression and torture was the best response. Whether the rebels and plotters were the poor or the rich … whether the causes were hunger or greed or belief … whether the goal was selfish or altruistic, they had to be suppressed.

> 'The ruthless economic exploitation and political oppression of the peasants by the landlord class forced them into numerous uprisings against its rule.'
>
> *Mao Tse Tung (1893–1976), Chinese political leader:*
> The Chinese Revolution *(December 1939)*

The Tudor monarchs were quirky and high profile. They were also high maintenance. And who paid for their rich reigns? The taxpayers. It's natural that the hard-working peasants grew angry at the injustice of being milked so the monarchs could get the cream.*

In the 1540s the poor suffered inordinately. Wages could not keep pace with inflation, and their real value fell by about 50 per cent over the decade. Labourers, living on a fixed income, suffered. Only large farmers profited. Of course the fat-cat farmers became a prime target for the disaffected poor.†

Kett's Rebellion

> 'War can only be abolished through war, and in order to get rid of the gun it is necessary to take up the gun.'
>
> *Mao Tse Tung*

In 1549 Young Edward VI was on the throne but the Protector, the Duke of Somerset, was the leader of the council and held the real power in England.

The peasants in Edward's England had watched as the landowners started shutting them out of the common land with hedges. In Norfolk the poor revolted. The rebels ripped out the hedges and demolished fences. Robert Kett, a 57-year-old farmer, was one of their targets. But instead of resisting the vandalism, he agreed with the peasant cause and offered to lead them.‡

* Headlines in 2014 say, 'Archbishop of Canterbury blasts fat-cat bankers'. Resentment at the greed of the great is alive and well 450 years on. *Plus ça change, plus c'est la même chose.*

† Except the fat-cat farmers weren't cat farmers … they were sheep farmers. Farming fat-cats has never been a profitable industry.

‡ Of course it wasn't that simple. History never is. In fact the rebels had targeted landowner Sir John Flowerdew. This practical man paid the rebels to go away and attack Robert Kett instead. An unusual tactic, but doomed to fail. After Kett tore down his own fences he led the peasants in tearing down Flowerdew's. Money can't buy you love.

The rebels had views quite close to a Marxist philosophy …

> 'The pride of great men is now intolerable, but our condition miserable.
>
> They abound in delights, but ourselves, almost killed with labour and watching, do nothing all our life long but sweat, mourn, hunger, and thirst.
>
> We desire liberty and an equal use of all things. This will we have. Otherwise these tumults and our lives shall only be ended together.'*
>
> *From Kett's* The Rebels' Complaint

Then Kett's rebels grew ambitious and attacked Norwich city, many armed with only with sticks and mud. The worried leaders of Norwich went out to meet Kett and sue for peace. They were met by a boy who dropped his trousers and showed them his backside.

Lord Sheffield's attempt to defend the city ended in black comedy. He fell from his horse into a ditch as he confronted the rebels. He removed his helmet to identify himself and surrender himself for ransom. A chivalric custom. The peasants didn't do chivalry. A butcher in the rebel ranks brained Sheffield's bare head.

The Protector, the Duke of Somerset, had underestimated the rebellion. Now he saw how serious it was he sent in an army under the Earl of Warwick, reinforced by 1,500 battle-hardened German mercenaries. The Protector wasn't the sort of man to sue for peace or negotiate. In the ensuing battle 3,000 of the 16,000 rebels died and Kett was captured; 49 rebels were hanged in Norwich.

---

* In other words, satisfaction or death. No prize coconuts for guessing which they achieved.

Kett was tortured in the Tower of London then sent back to be hanged from the side of Norwich Castle and left to rot in chains.

The Prayer Book Rebellion

> 'Dear Jesus, do something.'
>
> *Vladimir Nabokov (1899–1977), Russian-born novelist:* Pale Fire

Meanwhile there was unrest in Devon and Cornwall too. A second consecutive bad harvest in 1549 brought hunger for many.

Protestant zealot King Edward VI had introduced a new prayer book and it was not popular in the Catholic-leaning south-west. The rebels planned to march on London to protest, but stalled at Exeter when they decided to besiege the government forces in the city. The avowed aims of the rebels were to restore Catholicism and to 'Kill all the gentlemen'.

The five-week delay while they laid siege to Exeter gave the Duke of Somerset time to gather an army to halt the rebellion. Predictably the reckoning was savage with rebels being pursued and hanged. Around 5,500 rebels died, so this was no small skirmish.* Nor was it fought to any chivalrous rules. One report said 900 bound-and-gagged prisoners had their throats slit in ten minutes. Edward's forces were pitiless in his defence. Elizabeth must have taken note.

Yet sometimes persecution causes resentment, not simple fear. Even Somerset's friends were disgusted by his cruelty.

---

* In 2007 the Bishop of Truro apologized and said the Church of England had made an enormous mistake. 5,500 mistakes in fact, Bish. The sadness is the Prayer Book Rebels are forgotten – their deaths equal around four unforgotten *Titanic* disasters. For a prayer book.

As we have seen, his implacable savagery even extended to sending his own brother, Tom Seymour, to the scaffold.

The sheer inhumanity of Somerset turned the world against him. Like monsters before, and monsters since, he probably didn't care.

> 'The best political weapon is the weapon of terror. Cruelty commands respect. Men may hate us. But, we don't ask for their love; only for their fear.'
>
> *Heinrich Himmler (1900–45), Commander of Hitler's SS*

— SPOTTED SICKNESS —

> 'The coward's weapon, poison.'
>
> *John Fletcher (1579–1625), Jacobean playwright*

Elizabeth grew up healthy until her teens. Then she suffered various maladies. Her highly strung temperament would have been even more stressed when Catherine Parr gave birth to a daughter before falling ill, probably from puerperal sepsis.

For in her fevered state she claimed …

> 'Those that be about me care not for me but stand laughing at my grief.'

The rant seemed to be directed at her husband – the buttock-slapping, princess-kissing lecher, Thomas Seymour. That naturally led to rumours of poisoning. And rumour is so very seductive.

What did Tom Seymour stand to gain from his wife's death? Well, he was then free to court Princess Elizabeth. She may have been only second in line to the throne, but King Edward VI was a sickly youth and Mary was a Catholic who might not prove acceptable to the English people.

Elizabeth was a good bet … plus she had that nubile body Tom seemed to fancy. Is there any evidence that he had such grand designs? Elizabeth's governess, Kat Ashley, was quick to push his suit. Kat purred in Elizabeth's ear and pointed out that Tom was free and single again and the 'noblest unmarried man in the kingdom'.*

Why was she pushing the princess into a marriage? Was terrible Tom urging her to act as a go-between? Was it a Tom-Kat plot?

Is there any evidence that Tom still lusted after Liz? There is indeed. He wrote to the princess enquiring if 'her great buttocks were grown any less or no'. Cheeky. Two months after his wife's death his mourning was over.† Elizabeth also had a £3,000 p.a. inheritance that Tom seemed to find every bit as attractive as her 15-year-old buttocks.

Elizabeth said, 'No.' It wouldn't be the last marriage proposal she would decline. Kat Ashley continued to nag the princess while the rumour mill went into overdrive. The mongers of gossip branded Tom Seymour a poisoning paedophile. More cruelly they told tales of a midwife being blindfolded and taken to deliver the baby of an anonymous

---

* In reality Edward VI was the 'noblest unmarried man in the kingdom', but as he was just coming up to his eleventh birthday he probably doesn't count … and as he was Elizabeth's half-brother that rules him out too. Kat Ashley had a point.

† Like a good gambler who spreads his bets, Tom Seymour was also considering a marriage with Elizabeth's older sister, first in line to the throne, Mary Tudor. He was a bit of a lad, wasn't he?

girl. The girl was Elizabeth, the baby was the offspring of Seymour and it was destroyed to keep the secret (or so they said). Like mother like daughter, they whispered.

> 'What is told in the ear of a man is often heard a hundred miles away.'
>
> *Chinese Proverb*

The rumours reached Elizabeth. She was obliged to testify against Seymour when he was accused of treason. But it was his amorous adventures she focused on, not his treacherous ones. She declared in a letter to the Lord Protector who ruled for Edward VI …

> 'There goeth rumours which be greatly against my honour and honesty; that I am in the Tower; that I am with child by my Lord Admiral (Thomas Seymour). These are shameful slanders.
>
> *Elizabeth, letter to Lord Protector*

Tom was summoned to appear before the council that managed the country until Edward VI came of age. He declared that he would thrust his dagger into anyone who laid hands on him. But the threat was hot air. He was taken to the Tower of London. Kat Ashley blabbed about the kissing and spanking episodes. Elizabeth was embarrassed … but being molested by a lord is not a treasonable offence.

Some of Tom's other activities *were* treasonable. His indiscretions with a princess made him deeply unpopular so the guilty verdict at his trial was a certainty. On 20 March 1549 he lost his head on Tower Hill.

Elizabeth was never in that sort of danger from their dangerous liaison, but it was a shocking wake-up call. Slap and tickle (literally in her case) can be fatal (literally in the case of Tom Seymour). He never stood a chance.

> 'As Macbeth said to Hamlet in *A Midsummer Night's Dream*, we've been done up like a couple of kippers.'
>
> *Del Trotter, character in TV series* Only Fools and Horses

– LITTLE ED –

> 'Treason doth never prosper, what's the reason? For if it prosper, none dare call it Treason.'
>
> *Sir John Harington*

Young King Edward VI never reached the age where he could rule unaided by the council. He didn't last long. Heir today, gone tomorrow.

Thomas Seymour became as indiscreet with Edward as he was with Elizabeth. He gave the young king extra pocket money and said the Duke of Somerset (Tom's brother the Protector) was too mean to keep Edward in royal style.

Tom said Edward was being made to be a 'beggarly king'. Tom Seymour was a worm in the bud of the royal council. You might say he was a fawning, obsequious, devious, wily, scheming, Machiavellian, smarmy self-seeker (if you had a thesaurus handy). And, as he tried to get Edward to sign a document that would dismiss his Protector brother, you could add 'back-stabbing'.

Then in 1549 Tom overreached himself. He wanted a quiet word with the young king. Having decided to creep to Eddie's room after dark, he took a loaded pistol and slipped through the king's private garden.* But Eddie had bolted his door and left his favourite little spaniel on guard outside.

As Seymour tried the door latch the dog jumped up and started yapping. Seymour panicked. He shot the dog. That shot brought the guards running … though you have to wonder what they were doing to let Uncle Tom get that close anyway.

Edward might have forgiven the man his sneaky, late-night trip but not the killing of his dog. When Uncle Tom Seymour was charged with 33 treasonable offences (dog-killing not included) he got the chop. Young Edward did not intercede … even though his pocket money dried up more suddenly than Tom Seymour's head on a pole.

Somerset levelled 1549

> 'Treason is a charge invented by winners as an excuse for hanging the losers.'
>
> *Stone and Edwards musical* 1776 *(character of Benjamin Franklin)*

The Duke of Somerset hadn't intervened to save his brother either. So it's hard to feel sorry when he landed up to his neck in trouble. In order to consolidate his power as Protector he snatched King Edward from his bed in Hampton Court and moved him to Windsor. A shock to the young king and one he never forgave.

Edward wrote …

> 'Methinks I am in prison.'

* You have to admit that taking a loaded pistol to visit your nephew is highly suspicious. You'd be arrested if you tried it. Take him a train set.

He thinks right. The rest of the country thought so too and Somerset was soon under attack from the jealous and the righteous.

First Somerset was blamed for the Devon/Cornwall and Norfolk riots. Why hadn't this so-called Protector acted swiftly when King Ed needed protection from the rebels?

> 'Every man of the council have misliked your proceedings ... would to God, that, at the first stir you had followed the matter hotly, and caused justice to be ministered in solemn fashion to the terror of others.'*
>
> *William Paget (1506–63), private secretary to Henry VIII*

Somerset was opposed by the other lords on the council, arrested and taken to the Tower. King Edward sounded a bit miffed when he listed his grievances against Somerset:

> 'Ambition, vainglory, entering into rash wars in mine youth, enriching himself of my treasure, following his own opinion, and doing all by his own authority.'

Aggrieved Edward may have felt hurt by Somerset, but not as hurt as Somerset when the axe landed on his neck. As Shakespeare put it so succinctly ...

> 'Though those that are betray'd
> Do feel the treason sharply, yet the traitor
> Stands in worse case of woe.'
>
> Cymbeline, *William Shakespeare*

---

* Nice to see 'terror' being advocated as a technique for dealing with troublemakers. Scare the hell out of them and make an example to would-be anarchists. A policy that the Tudors followed gleefully. Negotiation? Pfffft! That's for wimps.

The Duke of Northumberland became the Protector of Edward, and Somerset's head followed his brother's to the straw beneath the block.

— DEAD ED 1553 —

> 'I fell sike of the mesels and smallpokkes.'
>
> *Edward VI's journal 1552*

Edward's medical diagnostic skills were better than his spelling.

It seems an attack of measles, which was quickly followed by a smallpox infection, set off an old case of tuberculosis. Edward recovered from the measles and smallpox. Big sister Elizabeth wrote to congratulate him on this 'good escape out of the perilous diseases'.

Her spelling was better than her diagnosis because Edward's demise was merely postponed. By the following January he had developed a cough and was weak. His doctors called it 'consumption', a common term for TB at the time. It was a messy business.

> 'The matter he ejects from his mouth is sometimes coloured a greenish-yellow and black, sometimes pink like the colour of blood.'
>
> *Seigneur de Rode-Saint-Agathe (1515–81), ambassador to the Holy Roman Empire*

Elizabeth was kept away from her dying brother while the new Protector, the Duke of Northumberland, plotted to put his own puppet on the throne ... Lady Jane Grey. Henry VIII had willed that, should Edward pop his clogs, the crown should pass to the children of his younger sister, not the bastards Mary or Elizabeth.

Edward VI was happy to reinforce his dad's will and name Lady Jane his successor – cutting Elizabeth and Mary out of the succession completely. The Duke of Northumberland quickly married off Jane Grey to his son and then waited for Edward to die.

Done and dusted. Everyone was happy … except 16-year-old Jane Grey, who was not at all keen on marrying the duke's son, Lord Guildford Dudley.

They just managed to beat the clock as they married on 21 May 1553 and Ed snuffed it eight weeks later. It was a reversal of Shakespeare's cynical jest…

> 'Thrift, thrift, Horatio! The funeral baked meats
> Did coldly furnish forth the marriage tables.'
>
> Hamlet, *William Shakespeare*

The last Tudor king was dead. Dead as a coffin nail.*

> 'The disease whereof his majesty died was the disease of the lungs, which had in them two great ulcers, and were putrefied, by means whereof he fell into consumption, and so hath he wasted, being utterly incurable.'
>
> *Cecil family papers*

Or DID he die from a lung disease? Rumours circulated. It was said that Northumberland fired Edward's doctors and

* Charles Dickens declared, in *A Christmas Carol*, that 'dead as a doornail' was an unsatisfactory phrase. 'I might have been inclined, myself, to regard a coffin-nail as the deadest piece of ironmongery in the trade,' he argued … and who are we to argue with the bearded Brit?

employed a 'wise woman'. The aim was to keep the young king alive long enough to arrange the marriage between Jane Grey and his son. The special potion she fed the fading king contained arsenic. It kept him alive … but kept him in agony at the same time.

Ed was in such pain he was praying to God to grant him the release of death. Then, when Ed nominated Lady Jane Grey as his successor and the marriage was consecrated, Northumberland was ready to let Edward die. The Protector sacked the wise woman and called the royal doctors back.*

Did you know … Tudor treatment

Edward VI's doctors made desperate attempts to save Ed's life. They mixed a potion containing:

- nine teaspoons of spearmint syrup
- turnip
- dates
- raisins
- celery
- pork from a nine-day-old sow

The ingredients were stirred into the spearmint sauce.

No wonder Edward VI's minister, William Cecil, said …

> 'God protect us from doctors.'

* There is even a story that Northumberland had the wise woman murdered. But if she was so very wise she'd have seen it coming and fled.

The common people were sure that Northumberland had poisoned Edward. Northumberland deflected the blame onto Mary. He said that last time Mary visited her brother 'she overlooked him with the evil eye of witchcraft'. (Northumberland was gambling with his life. He was going to be in trouble if Mary ever took the throne.)

A modern doctor can explain that Edward's death had all the symptoms of tuberculosis …

DANGEROUS DAYS DEATH II

TUBERCULOSIS

Tuberculosis (TB) is caused by the bacteria Mycobacterium tuberculosis. You generally catch it from the spit and snot of someone carrying the disease, but can also get it from infected milk. It only needs you to inhale around ten of the little blighters to get infected.

Once in the lungs the infection starts. The bacteria multiply causing the body to react and form a granuloma. This is a collection of decayed tissue, bacteria and your defending white cells. It looks like white, soft cheese, can burst into your windpipes and then be coughed up. It smells horrible.

Spreading elsewhere via the blood the infection slowly takes hold. The main symptoms are a bloody cough, a sweaty fever and pains from wherever the infection spreads to. Over time you lose weight and become very tired. Gradually over several months, sometimes years, you deteriorate, fading away and dying.

Dr Peter Fox

If you want an even more outrageous rumour there was a tale that Edward died *before* Northumberland had his army assembled, ready to enforce the succession of Jane Grey. He had to make Edward *appear* to be alive for a little longer. He delayed the announcement of the king's death. Then he had an Edward lookalike smothered and the fresh corpse substituted for the king's.

The fresh corpse was displayed to the public to show there was no obvious foul play. The real Edward's mouldering corpse was buried secretly in the grounds of Greenwich Palace while the substitute is the one now buried in Westminster Abbey.

With Lady Jane Grey jumping the queue, Elizabeth was still two heartbeats away from the crown. But Jane was a tragic figure who was destined to die.

— JANE, THE NINE-DAY WONDER —

> 'Those who plot the destruction of others often perish in the attempt.'
>
> *Thomas Moore (1779–1852), Irish poet*

Edward was a dead-ward and the Duke of Northumberland made his move. He summoned Mary and Elizabeth to the funeral. Mary set off then was warned she was riding into a trap. (Yes, you'd have thought she could have worked that out for herself.)

Elizabeth, the savvy sister, didn't set out at all. 'Sorry, Northumberland, I'm too ill to go to London,' she sighed.*

---

* In a curious twist of fate a subsequent Duke of Northumberland would,

Mary fled to Norfolk with a handful of attendants. Lady Jane Grey was proclaimed queen. But Northumberland was not popular. Mary was held in affection by the people of England … the Catholic fly in her ointment could be overlooked.

> 'The public is the only critic whose opinion is worth anything at all.'
>
> *Mark Twain (1835–1910), American author and humorist*

The people rallied to her cause and Northumberland marched from London to confront these upstarts.

— MARY: AVENGING LIAR —

Mary knew the English people would not be happy with a Catholic queen. When some Protestants from Cambridge found that she had spent the night in a nearby house they burned the place down. A hint to Mary perhaps, but also rather ironic since she would use burning to more devastating effect.

So what could Mary do to win the support of the Protestants? She said (no doubt with her fingers crossed behind her back) …

> 'The religion of England will not change very much from my brother's reign.'

---

some years later, decline an invite from Elizabeth to come to London when he feared it was a trap. It was. Show me Stalin's grave and I'll show you a Communist plot.

Gentlemen and peasants formed an army of 15,000 to march on London in Mary's support. The Duke of Northumberland marched out to meet that army. And what did the Londoners do as soon as Northumberland left? Rebelled, of course, and added *their* support to Mary's cause. The English fleet defected to her too. Northumberland's soldiers were enthusiastic looters but less keen on fighting his battles.

The Council in London gave her their allegiance and proclaimed Mary Tudor Queen of England. They wrote to her to say, in effect, 'We Londoners were always behind you – we kept quiet "to avoid any bloodshed". But now Northumberland has marched off we can declare our undying, enduring and eternal love for you, grovel, creep, crawl and fawn.'

In the streets the citizens of London celebrated with …

- ringing bells
- money thrown out of windows
- water fountains filled with wine
- bonfires
- feasting, dancing and singing in the streets
- caps thrown in the air

Mary was happy to accept their offer of support.

Even little Jane Grey said she was happy. She said …

> 'I am very glad I am no longer queen.'

She wasn't exactly throwing her crown in the air but, in a few months' time, she'd be able to throw her head in the air … it's just that she wouldn't be able to catch it.

And those bonfires would be lit under Protestants when Mary broke her promise to them.

Elizabeth recovered suddenly – there's no medicine like having the threat of death lifted. She entered London and waited for Mary to return from Norfolk. Happy Families was the name of the game – unless you were in the Northumberland branch, of course.

The Duke of Northumberland was in Cambridge when he heard that Londoners had deserted him and his daughter-in-law. What could he do? He went into the market square with a cap full of gold coins. He threw the cap in the air, scattering the coins while he declared, 'God save Queen Mary.'

The plebs scrambled for the coins while his friends noticed that Northumberland was crying.

His followers ripped the Northumberland badge off their coats and sneaked off home. Northumberland was taken to the Tower of London, where he joined Lady Jane Grey and his son. The mob threw mud, horse droppings and human droppings at him as he was led through the streets.

Jane had entered the Tower as her royal palace – she was now in there as a prisoner.

Mary made another one of those treacherous Tudor promises …

> 'I will spare the life of Lady Jane Grey.'

Northumberland was the first to go. He wriggled like an eel on a hook to avoid execution, weeping and pleading, even lying. He claimed he'd always been a good Catholic.

The judges passed sentence. Having been found guilty of treason, he was to be hanged, drawn and quartered. They added the tasty little line …

> 'His heart is to be cut from his body and flung in his face.'

A couple of weeks later he climbed onto the scaffold watched by 10,000 people who hated his guts. He made a final speech in which he admitted …

> 'I have deserved a thousand deaths.'

He only got one.

TORTURE AND TERROR

— FLAMING MARY —

> 'Power and tyranny have sometimes more force than right or justice.'
>
> *Simon Renard (1513–73), ambassador to Philip I of Spain and advisor to Mary Tudor*

So Catholic Mary took the throne. England was about to be plunged into a brief period of fear and uncertainty. It was nothing to the uncertainty of Elizabeth's situation. She would experience many dangerous days in her life but these were to be as close as she came to entertaining the executioner.

Political wisdom (and History) said to Mary, 'Kill her.' Vengeance said that she was the daughter of the detested Anne Boleyn ... 'Kill her.'

But ...

> 'Sister is probably the most competitive relationship within the family, but once the sisters are grown, it becomes the strongest relationship.'
>
> *Margaret Mead (1901–78), American cultural anthropologist*

Elizabeth played every card she knew in a poker game of survival. She suggested Mary send her Catholic books or a Catholic tutor to show her the error of her ways. Mary swallowed this act of a humble penitent. The tutor, Spanish ambassador Simon Renard, found the princess had an upset stomach when he came to instruct her. He wasn't convinced. Renard would express his anger later.

Nor was the French king's ambassador, Antoine de Noailles, swallowing the penitent act when he snorted …

> 'Everyone believes she is acting rather from fear of danger and peril from those around her than from real devotion.'

Spot on, Antoine … but most of us would do the same in Elizabeth's precarious situation.

Simon Renard would prove even more fiercely antagonistic towards Elizabeth … it was payback time for her slithering out of his religious tuition. He would have liked to see her disposed of permanently, and told Mary …

> 'Do not trust your sister who might conceive some dangerous design and put it to execution. It would be difficult to prevent as she is clever and sly …'
>
> *Simon Renard*

Renard was Mary's trusted friend. He was also advisor to Philip I of Spain. So what do we think Simon Renard's advice to Mary would be? That's right: 'Marry Philip. Make him King of England – unite the countries and have powerful armed forces at your command.'

Curiously, Renard reported that 'dangerous and sly' Princess Elizabeth was seated in a window as he negotiated a Spanish marriage with Mary. What must she have been thinking as she eavesdropped?

Henry VIII's niece, Margaret Douglas, was at that meeting too. And Margaret Douglas was Mary's preferred heir. No doubt Elizabeth could see her place in the queue for the throne being leapfrogged yet again … first by the birth of Edward, then by Jane Grey, then by her cousin Margaret and potentially by a child of big sister Mary. Always one step forward then one step back.

When Elizabeth attended Mary's coronation, Renard was convinced the princess was plotting with the French ambassador against Mary. A rumour went around that Elizabeth said, 'My coronet is too heavy.' The French ambassador chuckled and retorted, 'Never mind, you'll soon be swapping it for a crown.'

And that execution's twitching axe inched ever closer.*
In a dark tantrum, Mary spat that it would be a disgrace if Elizabeth inherited the throne …

> 'She is a heretic, a hypocrite and a bastard.'†

* All right, we are living in the metric age. The pedant may prefer to say, 'The axe centimetred ever closer.'

† This was reported in a Spanish journal and they were just a teensy bit prejudiced. Did she *really* say that?

The loving older sister blew hot and cold – Equatorial to Arctic, in fact. On another occasion she muttered her belief that Elizabeth wasn't even Henry VIII's daughter … that she resembled the musician Mark Smeaton.

And that insult was more than even the 'clever and sly' Elizabeth could bear. She asked to be excused from court. Renard raged, 'If she wants to leave then send her to the Tower.' Mary refused, but Elizabeth was demoted in the hierarchy at court; Margaret Douglas was given precedence in the ceremonies. That was adding to the insult. Even Lady Jane Grey's mother was given precedence – the mother of a convicted traitor.

Too much. Elizabeth sulked. She did her 'I'm-too-poorly-to-attend' act. At last the princess was allowed to retire to Ashridge. But she would be watched. Any hint of plotting would be fatal.

Elizabeth's enemies were dangerous. But her 'friends' – anyone who pushed her towards the throne – could be deadly.

> 'True friends stab you in the front.' *Oscar Wilde*

Cold-footed favourite – Edward Courtenay 1553

> 'Those traits we detest, sharpness, greed, acquisitiveness, meanness, egotism and self-interest, are the traits of success.'
>
> *John Steinbeck (1902–68), American author*

The Catholics were back in power and Edward's religious laws were all reversed. So would the monks get their lands and monasteries back? Of course not. Those were in the tight fists of the wealthy; giving the bones of the monasteries to the wealthy Rottweilers had been easy – but not even Mary was going to prise them free from those jaws again.

The best way for Mary to cement her power was to marry a powerful Catholic. The most eligible and desirable was Philip of Spain. Mary herself was half-Spanish and she wanted to keep it in the family. Mary's English subjects had learned to loathe the Spanish, but the lady was not for turning. It was God's will, she believed ... and one God outweighed millions of English xenophobic whingers.*

But there were English alternatives. A young relative of the last Plantagenet king, Richard III, was suggested as a suitable match. He was Edward Courtenay, second cousin to Elizabeth. Mary liked Courtenay and was great friends with his mother. She rejected the idea of marrying him because Philip of Spain was a far bigger catch.

But Mary's enemies had a sensational idea ... marry Edward Courtenay to Elizabeth.

The younger princess was more likely to produce an heir, and Courtenay, being English, would meet with the approval of the rebels who cried ...

> 'We are all Englishmen. We will have no foreigner for our king.'†

---

* English opposition to the Spanish marriage was expressed on New Year's Day 1554 when servants from the Spanish Embassy were attacked by Londoners. With snowballs. That's not an ice welcome is it?

† Rather conveniently forgetting the Tudor family was Welsh. Maybe a Welsh woman can become an honorary Englishman when it suits the nationalists?

Mary had generously made Courtenay Earl of Devonshire so, the malcontents reckoned, he and Princess Elizabeth could go to the West Country and organize a rebellion against the queen.

There were two flaws with this cunning plot. Firstly, Elizabeth wasn't party to it … or if she was it hasn't been recorded. And Edward himself was too much of a wuss to agree to a rebellion.

Or three flaws in truth. Courtenay himself declared that marrying Elizabeth would be *beneath* him. He was from the noble line of the Plantagenet family who had lost power when Richard III lost his horse. Someone must have told him that the Plantagenets were yesterday's news, but he still had delusions of self-importance. Commentators said he was rather a dim young man. It shows.

Imagine that? You have a chance to change history and you bottle it. Courtenay had nothing to lose … except his head, not to mention his intestines, his genitalia and his limbs when he was hanged, drawn and quartered.

> COWARDLY LION: [crying] 'I am a coward! I haven't any courage at all. I even scare myself. Look at the circles under my eyes. I haven't slept in weeks!'
> TIN WOODSMAN: 'Why don't you try counting sheep?'
> COWARDLY LION: 'That doesn't do any good, I'm afraid of 'em.'
>
> *Dialogue from* The Wizard of Oz *movie (1939)*

The plotters had come up with an Elizabethan plot, unsought by the princess, and put her in danger of her life. Despite Courtenay's cold feet, a rebellion WAS brewing in Cornwall as well as other counties. It wouldn't be led by the Duke of Devonshire, but it would tangle Elizabeth in its web.

MARY: RUTHLESS RULER

> 'Never doubt that a small group of thoughtful, committed citizens can change the world. Indeed, it is the only thing that ever has.'
>
> *Margaret Mead*

When Edward VI died, Princess Elizabeth, aged 20, had been happily reunited with big sister Mary, aged 37. The cloud in the silver lining was Jane Grey. The nine-day queen Jane was told she would stand trial and be found guilty, but not to worry, Queen Mary would spare her life. The 15-year-old ex-queen was pleased and said,

> 'She is a merciful queen.'

Jane Grey had Tudor blood herself – she should have known better than to believe Mary's good-will words. Or maybe Mary meant it when she said it.

But a rebel rising, led by Sir Thomas Wyatt of Kent, spoiled it all. The big fear in England was that if Mary married King Philip of Spain it would open the door of England to the Spanish and their fearsome Inquisition … which Mary did, of course.*

Wyatt organized anti-Catholic forces to converge on London. One of the rebel forces was led by Lady Jane's father; obviously he wanted to put Lady Jane on the throne. The

* Philip argued that the Spanish Inquisition didn't burn a single heretic to death. Not one. And, technically, that was true. When the Church found the victims guilty, it duly handed them over to the civil authorities and the government burned them. Either way, you'd end up cremated.

Devon contingent shrivelled away when Edward Courtenay failed to support the rising.

The men of Kent found themselves alone. Their averred aim must chime with today's British National Party (poster slogan, 'British jobs for British workers'). It was (according to one rebel) …

> 'To prevent us from over-running with strangers.'

Wyatt and his fellow conspirators planned to descend on London in March 1554, in time to crash the wedding of Mary and Philip. But, as ever, someone blabbed and the unready rebels had to strike immediately.* The rising began in late January 1554.

The rebellion failed.† In the narrow London streets Wyatt's 4,000 warriors were ambushed from alleys and smashed by the locals. A glorious confirmation that guerrilla tactics can defeat the most determined and skilled army.

> 'Two hundred men can defeat six hundred when the six hundred behave like fools. When they forget the very conditions they are fighting in … when they fight in streets without remembering the object of streets … advancing into the bowels of a fortress, with streets pointing at you, streets turning on you, streets jumping out at you, and all in the hands of the enemy.'
>
> The Napoleon of Notting Hill, *G.K. Chesterton*

---

* It may have been the timid Edward Courtenay who betrayed the plotters. He would hope for mercy if the rebellion failed … and hope no one found out he'd snitched if the rebels succeeded.

† The force assembled in the Midlands numbered just 140. A good rugby team armed with baseball bats could have put a stop to their game.

As Wyatt advanced down Fleet Street the rebels' lines were attacked from the side streets and chopped like a worm under a gardener's spade. Wyatt surrendered. His future was not looking bright.

Mary's chancellor and spy chief, Stephen Gardiner, suspected the French were involved in supporting Wyatt, so his henchmen did a little highway robbery to intercept the French ambassador's messages home. The letters *did* implicate the French but, by chance, they found a letter from Elizabeth to the French king. It wasn't a particularly incriminating letter but it WAS proof of contact with a dangerous foreign power.

Elizabeth had been claiming illness to avoid confinement in London. The princess certainly *was* ill at the time, but as in the case of the boy who cried wolf, she was not believed. Her sister's patience was now thin as a butterfly's wing; Mary sent a posse to bring her, sick or well, 'quick or dead'. Elizabeth was carried back to London, through city gates that were decorated with the heads and quarters of traitors. She must have wondered if she'd be joining the crow-pecked bones very soon. *Memento mori.*

> 'For a few moments, the secrets of the universe are opened to us. Life is a cheap parlour trick. That's the miserable truth.'
>
> *Jonathan Nolan (1976—),*
> *British-American author and screenwriter*

As she travelled to house-arrest in Whitehall, Elizabeth received shocking and ominous news. The 'merciful queen' had reneged on her merciful promise.

Mary and her ministers had decided that the best way to stop any more rebellions like Wyatt's would be to execute Jane Grey and her husband. By the time Elizabeth reached

London, Lady Jane's little life was extinguished. At least Jane didn't grovel like her father-in-law Northumberland. Instead she said …

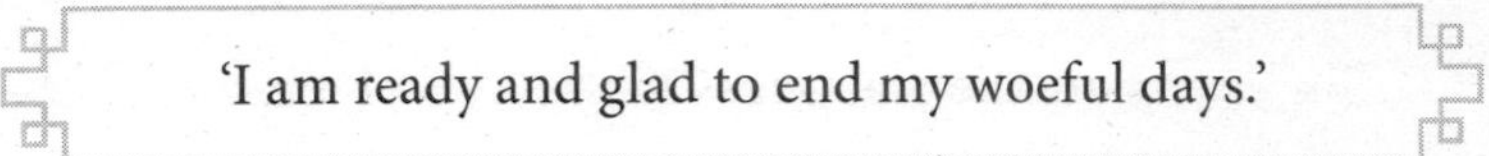

> 'I am ready and glad to end my woeful days.'

It's strange that the two Tudor women to die on the block (Jane Grey and Mary, Queen of Scots, 30 years later) both died bravely. Jane's father-in-law, Northumberland, had begged for his life, her rebel father had pleaded for mercy and his son (her husband) was 'in a state of collapse, weeping and angry about his unkind fate'. An axe on the back of his neck dried his sobbing faster than an absorbent tissue.

Jane followed him to the scaffold and acted out a scene that would have been comical if it hadn't been so gruesome. The executioner showed her the block. She knelt down and tied a handkerchief over her own eyes. But, once she was blindfolded, she couldn't remember where the block was. She waved her hands about wildly calling, 'What shall I do? Where is it?'

After an agonising wait someone guided her hands to the block and she laid her neck on it. Moments later her freckled face hit the straw.

She died well.

— SAVAGE SISTER —

> 'Big sisters are the crab grass in the lawn of life.'
>
> *Charles M. Schulz (1922–2000), American cartoonist: Charlie Brown,* Peanuts

Jane Grey's father may have been a leading rebel, but Wyatt himself had declared that his aim was to put Elizabeth on the throne. Mary had disposed of rival Jane and now turned her fury upon Elizabeth.

Wyatt was tortured before his execution but refused to admit Elizabeth herself had endorsed his treason. He had sent her letters to inform her of his progress, but there was no solid evidence that she encouraged him or had expectations of the crown.

Elizabeth protested her loyalty to Mary and said she had never supported Wyatt and his cronies. The princess was articulate and ardent in her own defence. Did Mary believe her? Perhaps … but not enough to take the risk. Renard the Spaniard ranted that the princess should at least be committed to the Tower. He had his way.

The barge came to take Elizabeth to the Tower, which had been her mother's last residence and whose halls she still haunted. She wrote to Mary. It was the last throw of the dice in the last chance saloon. If she got the letter wrong then it would be her head, not dice, that would be rolling.

You could write the letter yourself, couldn't you? It wasn't me, Sis. I'm innocent as the day is long. Would I do such a thing? Etc. – but in more formal language …

> 'I am commanded to go to the Tower, a place more wonted for a false traitor than a true subject. I protest afore God that I never practised, counselled nor consented to anything that might be prejudicial to your person in any way.'

She asked for a hearing *before* she was sent to the haunting Tower. The letter (full of crossings-out and errors in Elizabeth's nervous state) was taken to Mary – same palace, different room.

The queen exploded with rage when she read the letter and realized it was a delaying tactic. She discovered her councillors had failed to carry her stepsister off to the Tower. Elizabeth's stalling meant the boat* to the Tower had missed the tide and she had manoeuvred her way into another night in Whitehall.

But it wasn't a reprieve. The next day she was rowed away to the false-traitors' prison. She shared her imprisonment with Edward Courtenay. She was held with the shadow of the executioner's sword always on the periphery of her mind's eye.

The Spanish envoy, Simon Renard, raged that it would not be safe for his master, Philip, to come from Spain until Elizabeth and Edward Courtenay had been executed.

How would Mary ensure Elizabeth was neutralized, he wondered? With an axe? Why not?

---

* A carriage journey through the streets could have upset the Londoners who admired Elizabeth. A riot or a rescue attempt might have followed.

 Princess Elizabeth was a focus for Protestant rebellion.

 Princess Elizabeth was a more attractive proposition than Mary as she was younger and more likely to bear an heir.

 Princess Elizabeth was a distant relative of the treacherous Wyatt family.*

Elizabeth landed at the Tower of London shouting her innocence to the guards and jailers.

> 'A woman is like a tea bag – you can't tell how strong she is until you put her in hot water.'
>
> *Eleanor Roosevelt (1884–1962), US First Lady*

How strong was Elizabeth? She sat down on the steps to Traitors' Gate and sulked. Remember that when, in later years, she boasted of her courage in the face of danger. Her 'bottle' was empty. She threw a terrified tantrum. Not so much Princess Elizabeth Tudor, more Violet Elizabeth Bott.†

* The Wyatts were ruined by the rebellion. When Elizabeth came to the throne she restored their lands and fortunes. Is that how you treat rebels? No. Is that how you treat martyrs to your cause? Ah, there's the question.

† For those not blessed with a classical education, Violet is a character in the *Just William* books by Richmal Crompton. She is the lisping, spoiled daughter of a local whose habitual threat to William is, 'I'll thcream and thcream 'till I'm thick.'

BRIEF TIMELINE – ELIZABETH THE HEIR

1550 A plague known as the sweating sickness strikes England.

1552 Ex-head of ruling council, the Duke of Somerset, becomes ex-head when it is sliced off on the block. Conservative Protestants are in the ascendancy.

1553 Sickly Edward VI makes a will naming cousin Lady Jane Grey (age 15) his successor. She has no powerful support. He is effectively signing her death warrant. Then he dies. Sister Mary (aged 37) puts an end to Jane's pretensions and to her neck.

1554 Rebellion led by Sir Thomas Wyatt. Elizabeth is arrested for allegedly supporting his cause. Mary marries Philip of Spain – a Catholic dynasty that they believe will rule for ever … or at least four years.

1555 Mary starts a Protestant purge with burnings at the stake. Hundreds of them. They will earn her the moniker 'Bloody Mary'.

1556 Famine, flu epidemic, inflation and starvation. Business as usual for the underclasses, but no rebellions this time.

1558 Mary dies. Elizabeth succeeds at the age of 25. All change back to Protestant.

1559 First in line to woo the new Queen Bess is Philip of Spain. She tells Parliament she has no plans to wed. Philip is eyeing that English throne. He never had the title King of England when he was married to Mary. But he'll be back …

— ELIZABETH'S DARKEST DAYS —

> 'Be nice to people on your way up because you'll meet the same people on your way down.'
>
> *Wilson Mizner (1876–1933), American playwright*

Elizabeth's jailers, under the command of the Earl of Sussex, were careful with their prisoner. They were fully aware that Elizabeth was the most likely heir to the throne. If they treated her badly, she would undoubtedly have her revenge.*

As Sussex put it bluntly …

> 'Let us use such dealing that we may answer it hereafter, if it shall so happen.'

Wise and prescient words. Oddly, the Constable of the Tower, Sir John Gage, was less considerate. He tried to force the princess to eat with the common herd. Gage was furious when she was allowed to have her own food and her own top cook. Then crafty sense prevailed; he reorganized the kitchens so he shared in Elizabeth's quality dining – at her expense – and he mellowed. Self-interest triumphs yet again.

Nice nosh or not, Elizabeth's spirits sank. The memories of her mother must have infected her dreams. She later confided that, if she faced execution, she would make one last desperate plea to Mary. Would the queen grant her the same humane French swordsman that had dealt so efficiently with her mother? She wanted to be a chip off the old non-block.

Easter 1554 came and went, as Easters tend to do, and still

---

* And if they treated her well would she reward them well? Probably not.

Renard fretted for the safety of his master, Philip. As ever, his answer was to press for the execution of Elizabeth and Courtenay. And, as ever, Mary procrastinated. It was time for Renard to deliver an ultimatum: deal with the pair of them or Philip won't be on the slow boat to Wapping.

Mary promised they would be brought to trial.

– THE FLATTERED FAVOURITE –

> 'My Lord, my client only went in to buy a seven-penny stamp. But as he was kept waiting by ten old ladies with pension books, he lost his patience and blew the safe.'
>
> *John Mortimer (1923–2009), British barrister and author: character Horace Rumpole*

There was a singular lack of evidence against Elizabeth and Courtenay. The one awkward question was about Elizabeth's orders to fortify Donnington Castle.

The rebel Wyatt was being kept alive in the hope he'd implicate Elizabeth in his plot. He said he had written to the princess and advised her to go to Donnington for her safety until Mary was overthrown. Elizabeth made plans to move to Donnington. Surely a sign that she was in touch with the rebels?

The accusation caught her unawares. She claimed, bizarrely, 'Donnington? Never heard of the place. I didn't even know I owned it.' Her reply was treated with scepticism. So she did what all bad children do and changed her story.

'Yes,' she admitted, 'I DO remember owning a place called Donnington … but I've never been there in my life and can't remember making any plans to go there.'

And THEN she remembered, 'Some of my household officers DID discuss a move to Donnington. So what? It's my house and I can go there if I want, can't I?'

She turned defence into attack. She was such an effective self-defence counsel she had one of the examining lords apologize to her. Lord Arundel, a pro-Spanish advocate, said ...

> 'We are very sorry to have troubled you with such vain matters.'

Elizabeth forgave him. How noble of her. Did Arundel have a sudden passion for the princess and fancy his chances of sharing the throne with her in time? Who knows? He was certainly touted as a suitor when she came to the throne.

And was Elizabeth aware of her power over a man like him? She batted her eyelashes and he fell.

But when Elizabeth succeeded to the throne, he kept his job (and his head). Maybe he wasn't such a soft touch after all.*

Did you know ... the Earl of Arundel

Arundel was not a trustworthy Tudor. In 1551 he had been imprisoned in the Tower, mainly through the machinations of Lady Jane Grey's father-in-law, the Duke of Northumberland. Arundel took his revenge on Northumberland by pretending to support him in

---

* As a Catholic he was involved in some of the major plots against Queen Elizabeth. He was arrested occasionally yet never lost his power or wealth. The fines and house arrests were just slaps on the wrist. Countless men and women died horribly for lesser offences and/or on lesser evidence. He should have been called ASBO Arundel.

the plot to make Lady Jane Grey queen. Then Arundel betrayed Northumberland to Queen Mary, and had the unalloyed joy of arresting his old enemy at Cambridge.

He said, 'I deny being drawn by any desire of revenge.' We believe you, Arundel.

He is credited with bringing the idea of horse-drawn carriages from France to England. Let's hope his axle-bearings were more reliable than his feigned friendship. It's a disputed claim, as is the assertion he gave Elizabeth the first silk stockings ever seen in England.

Elizabeth was cross-examined and Chancellor Stephen Gardiner found himself agreeing with Ambassador Renard. Elizabeth had to die to secure the kingdom. As soon as there was proof of her complicity with Wyatt, she'd be dead meat. The Grim Reaper was sharpening his scythe for Elizabeth.

> 'But at my back I always hear
> Time's wingèd chariot hurrying near.'
>
> *Andrew Marvell (1621–78), English poet*

Still Renard nagged and still the evidence refused to accumulate.

— MARRIED MARY —

> 'Much suspected by me,
> Nothing proved can be.'
>
> *Princess Elizabeth: allegedly scratched on a glass windowpane in her Woodstock prison*

Rebel Wyatt was executed after a speech, on the scaffold, where he exonerated Elizabeth of any part in his uprising. Yet still the princess Elizabeth remained in the Tower under a cloud of suspicion.

The English people were as hostile to Philip's arrival as ever. They left little tokens of their animosity – like a cat, dressed in the robes of a Catholic priest and hanged on a London gallows.

There was a scandal about a 'voice in the wall'. If you spoke to the wall of this mystical, empty house and said, 'God save Queen Mary,' it stayed silent as a brick. But if you said, 'God save Queen Elizabeth,' the wall replied, 'So be it.' A miracle? A God-given sign … or a fraud?

> 'How often have I said to you that when you have eliminated the impossible, whatever remains, however improbable, must be the truth?'
>
> *Arthur Conan Doyle (1859–1930), Scottish doctor and writer: character Sherlock Holmes in* The Sign of Four

Crowds up to 10,000 strong had gathered to witness this affirmation of Elizabeth's right. It turned out to be a servant girl who concealed herself in the empty house.*

* When discovered, the girl was locked in a pillory every day for several months as a lesson to others. Mystery one day, misery the next.

Talking walls made Elizabeth's life expectancy seem akin to that of a hanged Catholic cat. But she was moved from the Tower to Woodstock while, in July 1554, Mary married the dashing Philip. In September, one of the queen's doctors declared that Mary was pregnant. She did seem to show many of the signs, including nausea and a swelling belly.

Mary was ecstatic. Philip began to make plans to ensure his succession to the throne of England if Mary died in childbirth. A practical man … if a little unsentimental.

The queen loved her young husband madly. He was never quite so keen. As some of his unkind (but honest) courtiers said when they arrived for the wedding:

> 'Mary is older than we had been told.* She is not at all beautiful and is small and flabby rather than fat. She has a white complexion, is fair and has no eyebrows.'

Others complained, 'She has lost most of her teeth' and 'She dresses very badly.'

Cruellest of all was the courtier who said, 'What shall the king do with such an old bitch?'

What did dashing Philip do? He dashed … off to Flanders to fight for Spain. 'I'll be back in six weeks,' he lied.

He came back over a year later for a short stay in 1557, then the French attacked Scarborough.† *Chacun à son goût*. It was the excuse the king-consort Philip needed to leave his black-toothed bride and he was gone like the wind under Superman's cape. Philip set off to attack France but

---

* How can a queen be 'older than we had been told'? Her birth would be a matter of record. Was she heavier than her weight? Was she taller than she looked?

† French King Henri denied his forces were responsible. Ooh-la-liar.

only succeeded in losing England's one remaining French foothold – Calais. It had been in English hands since 1347 and it took a Spaniard to lose it. Thanks, Phil. As Mary put it so dramatically …

> 'When I am dead and opened up, you shall find Calais lying in my heart.'

— BLAME AND FLAME —

> 'No kingdom has ever had as many civil wars as the kingdom of Christ.'
>
> *Montesquieu (1689–1755), French social commentator*

Mary will be for ever remembered as Bloody Mary. Did she deserve that accolade?

Mary was miserable. And every time she got miserable she decided she must have upset God. So, to make God happy, she burned more and more heretics. A miserable Mary was a murderous Mary.

As Mary's confidence grew, she went beyond restoring the Catholic religion. She began killing the most stubborn Protestants. And, as they were 'heretics', they were burned alive. Burning was meant to cleanse the unbeliever's body and renew their soul. Persecutors such as Mary almost certainly saw burning as a sort of kindness for heretics.

Under Mary, 300 Protestants were burned at the stake between 1555 and 1558. Two a week experienced Mary's 'kindness'.

Of course, the death was a long, agonising and slow one,

but the sinful flesh would be burnt and the soul would escape – clean and free from sin. That was the theory.

In Oxford in 1555 Mary had Bishop Latimer and Bishop Ridley burned at the stake. Old Latimer was 70 years old. He made the most of his martyr's death by leaving behind one of those quotes that is remembered long after his persecutors are forgotten. He turned to Ridley alongside him and said …

> 'Play the man, Master Ridley; we shall this day light such a candle, by God's grace, in England, as I trust shall never be put out.'

And his optimism was justified. The Protestants would soon be ruling – and the persecuting boot would be on the other metatarsals.

Latimer and Ridley went to a quiet execution. There was none of the jeering and abuse that criminals usually suffered on their way to the Tudor gallows. At the same time there was no shortage of ghoulish voyeurs who enjoyed watching a fellow human's suffering and death.

The executioner tied a bag of gunpowder around each prisoner's neck – the explosion would (theoretically) kill them and reduce the suffering. (How generous of Mary to permit that.) But in many such executions the bags were damp fireworks that sizzled and scorched and exacerbated the agony.

It worked for Latimer. But this was mid-October and Ridley's sticks were a bit on the damp side. They smoked a lot. They burned slowly … and so did Ridley. 'I cannot burn,' he wailed. The screams must have given the ghouls a few nightmares. A guard pulled away some of the damp wood. The flames leapt up and detonated the bag of gunpowder round the bishop's neck and brought him a merciful release.

At last the ropes burned through and he fell forward into the fire. Of course the executioner had to push the bits back in the flames.

— THE RELUCTANT KINDLING —

> 'I assess the power of a will by how much resistance, pain, torture it endures and knows how to turn to its advantage.'
>
> *Friedrich Nietzsche*

> 'If it had been me they could have tortured me for years without getting anything out of my pain-racked body. "Do your damndest," I'd have shouted. "My lips are sealed. Put me on the rack, stretch my joints to the utmost. Pull my teeth out one by one without any anaesthetic and I'll still be smiling" … oh, no, I won't.'
>
> *Character Commander Murray in* The Navy Lark, *April 1972*

When, the following year, it was the turn of Thomas Cranmer, Archbishop of Canterbury, to go to the stake, he lost his nerve. 'I'll become a Catholic!' he wailed.

'Sign this paper to show you mean it,' his tormentors told him.

Cranmer signed. They smiled and said, 'Thanks. Now we're going to burn you anyway.' He was led to the university church in Oxford to reaffirm his return to the Catholic fold. But Cranmer was miffed. Instead he began to rant *against* the Catholics …

> 'As for the pope, I refuse him, as Christ's enemy.'

Mary's embarrassed officers hurried him away to the stake.

As the fire sprang upwards he stretched out his right hand – the hand that had signed the paper – as if he wanted to punish the hand for being so wicked.*

Cranmer's gesture was a powerful symbol. The execution was something of a propaganda disaster for Mary.

To the Protestants, Latimer, Ridley and Cranmer were heroes – people who'd died for their religion. In the 1800s a Martyrs' Cross was put up in St Giles, Oxford, to commemorate them. A cross on the road marks the spot where they were burned in Broad Street. In the church, where holes were made in the pillars to hold the scaffold, there is a plaque honouring the Oxford martyrs.

They are remembered. Maybe Latimer was right when he said, 'We shall light such a candle it shall never be put out.'

Less well remembered are the Stratford martyrs – Stratford in London, not Shakespeare's birthplace. Eleven men and two women were burned for heresy in 1556. Foxe, in his *Book of Martyrs*, added the unusual detail …

> 'Eleven men were tied to three stakes, and the two women loose in the midst without any stake; and so they were all burnt in one fire.'

The women may have been rendered insensible by being (mercifully) strangled. But again the statistic that shocks is the estimate of the number of Londoners who turned up to watch others die a hideous death. Twenty thousand

---

* Of course this is seriously stupid. It was his *brain* that told his hand to sign. Why didn't he fry his brain? Poor helpless hand.

spectators. Only half the number of Romans who flocked to the Coliseum to watch the murders in the arena, but still an insight into our fairly recent ancestors.

Their blood-lust was soon sated. In 45 murderous months from February 1555 to November 1558, 227 men and 56 women died for their Protestant faith and in London the crowds were becoming sickened by the smell of burning flesh.

For the last six months the burnings were conducted in secret locations to reduce the risk of riots. Mary had overplayed her hand.

DANGEROUS DAYS DEATH III

HANGED, DRAWN AND QUARTERED

The hanged bit is straightforward. Hands tied behind your back, naked, you hang from a rope. It tightens around your neck, closing off your windpipe and starving you of oxygen. As you fight to breathe, your brain starts to run out of oxygen. Just as you black out, the rope is cut and you fall to the ground. Gasping for air, slowly you regain consciousness.

The executioner then cuts off your penis and testicles – hopefully with a sharp blade. Though eye-wateringly painful, a tad bloody and definitely life-changing, it's not fatal, so you are well aware of his next 'surgery' as he opens up your abdomen. Reaching in, he removes your intestines and cuts them up, before tossing them onto a fire. You watch them burn just as the accumulated blood loss causes oxygen starvation to the brain and you lose consciousness again.

This means you fortunately miss the beheading and quartering finale where you die.

Dr Peter Fox

— THE PERILS OF PLOTTING —

In 1556 Mary was alone, Philip had gone and Parliament was hostile. The miserable monarch faced another plot. The plan, according to Henry Dudley, ringleader, was …

> 'To send Mary into exile with her husband, or dispose of her more permanently, and make the Lady Elizabeth queen.'
>
> *Henry Dudley (1517–68), English Tudor conspirator*

Elizabeth must have shuddered when she heard of the plot. It was the Wyatt problem all over again. She'd be suspected. If the plot was defeated – as they always were – then her neck would be measured for the block.

The French were deeply involved but the English gentry were rather lukewarm in their support for Henry Dudley. The cheeky part of the plot was that the funds to pay a mercenary force were to be stolen from the queen's own treasury. Henry Peckham, son of Sir Edward Peckham, Master of the Tower Mint, was caught red-handed. He was hanged, along with co-conspirators, and his head removed then hoisted to decorate London Bridge.

The plot failed in May 1556 and Mary reassured her sister she was not under suspicion. But the plots grew pottier. By July a schoolteacher called Cleobury was claiming to be the exiled Edward Courtenay. This clownish, counterfeit-Courtenay told a Suffolk church congregation that Mary was dead. He proclaimed Elizabeth as queen and himself – Elizabeth's 'beloved bedfellow' – as king. He didn't have a lot of credibility and failed to stir or a hornet's nest … or even a small bird's nest. He was executed.*

* And so was the parish priest where the treasonable declaration was made. A vicious way to treat a vicar.

Elizabeth grovelled in a letter to Mary. She was sorry her name had been used (again) in a plot of which she had no knowledge …

> 'If surgeons could make anatomies of the heart you would see, in mine, that I have been your faithful subject from the beginning of your reign. No wicked person shall cause me to change to the end of my life.'

Or the end of Mary's life, of course.

Plots against Mary grew curiouser and curiouser. In September 1556 rumours began to circulate of a new plot that could have come straight from the script of a 'Carry on Plotting' movie. A Frenchman was going to land secretly. He would vary his disguise as he travelled from town to town proclaiming Mary dead and Elizabeth queen. To avoid detection, he'd appear one day as a peasant, the next as a traveller, the next as a merchant. He would then disappear into the forests of England to hide.

In order to thwart his Pimpernel plot, the authorities armed themselves with bloodhounds – he may change his appearance but he couldn't disguise his smell. (You couldn't make it up.)

Mary was tolerant but still wanted Elizabeth shackled to a man in marriage. Courtenay died mysteriously in exile in Padua. But other suitors were hawked like bananas on a barrow-boy's cart. The latest were …

Philip's cousin, Emmanuel Philibert, Prince of Piedmont and Duke of Savoy – Elizabeth burst into tears when Mary proposed this and claimed she never wanted to marry. Mary took that as a 'No'.

Eric, son of King Gustavus of Sweden – Elizabeth said, 'I have never heard of His Majesty before this time.' Ouch.

But Mary was upset because the Swedish envoy went straight to Elizabeth when he should have conducted negotiations through head barrow-boy, Mary.

– UNMOURNED MARY –

Philip never returned from his French venture and that left Mary heartbroken. She was convinced in 1558 that she was pregnant again at the age of 42. It was a false alarm – a phantom pregnancy.

In March that year Mary drafted her will with a child in mind as her heir. But, by April, no child had come and Mary was left quite ill.

She declined quickly. In late October the queen drifted in and out of consciousness, but was lucid enough to pass the crown to her half-sister.

At around the same time, Philip learned of the death of both his father and his aunt. He was King of Spain and had the delusion he was rightful King of England too.

Did you know … I only have pies for you, dear

Mary was so desperate to get Philip back to England, she ordered her cooks to send his favourite meat pies across to Flanders. 'The way to a man's heart is through his stomach', they used to say.

As Mary lay dying she sent messengers to her sister Elizabeth to say it had 'pleased the Lord God' to end her days. She acknowledged Elizabeth would succeed her and begged her heir to keep the country Catholic. Elizabeth must have been tempted to say the Tudor equivalent of, 'In your dreams, Mary.'

Instead, equivocating as ever, she replied …

> 'I promise this much, that I will not change it so long as it can be proved by the word of God, which shall be the only foundation and rule of my religion.'

Meaning she would find every excuse to make the country revert to the Protestant religion once more.

Mary from her deathbed went on burning Protestants as enthusiastically as ever. By June it was recorded that they were 'now burning in Smithfield seven on one fire'.

On 11 November the last Protestant martyrs went to their dreadful deaths. Mary grew too sick to sign more death warrants. The register of martyrs ends …

> 'Six days after these were burned to death God sent us our *Elizabeth*.'

On 17 November, Mary died. The queen is dead, long live the queen. Elizabeth was at Hatfield when the news came and she couldn't contain her joy, declaiming …

> 'This is the Lord's doing and it is marvellous in our eyes.'

There was little in the way of mourning from the English people and Elizabeth was too preoccupied with securing the crown to spend time grieving. 'Our Elizabeth' would carry on murdering, simply switching the victims. Elizabeth's days would be as dangerous as ever for some poor souls.

But there were increasing dangers for Elizabeth herself now that she was the tallest poppy in the weed-infested field of English life.

CHOP AND CHANGE

— ELIZABETH THE QUEEN —

> 'I would rather sleep in the southern corner of a little country churchyard than in the tomb of the Capulets. I should like, however, that my dust should mingle with kindred dust.'
>
> *Edmund Burke (1729–97), Irish statesman, philosopher*

The hypocrisy of death makes enemies appear united. The brutal truth is that Mary died and her tomb in Elizabeth's reign became buried under piles of stone from broken altars.

Elizabeth herself died, as everyone does, and her successor, James I, built a fine tomb for both sisters. The skeletons must still be spinning if not sparring. A Latin plaque reads…

> 'Partners both in throne and grave, here rest we two sisters, Elizabeth and Mary, in the hope of one resurrection.'

Unlikely, James my boy.

The religious pendulum had swung back to Protestants.

Did you know ... dreadful Don Carlos

Philip of Spain had married his cousin, Maria of Portugal, in 1543 when they were both 16. She gave birth to a son, Don Carlos, but she died a few days later.

If Philip had become King of England, Don Carlos may have inherited. England had a lucky escape. For Don Carlos was a sad and sickly child. He grew up hunchbacked and pigeon-breasted with shoulders of uneven height and his right leg a lot shorter than the left.

Before he was 5 years old deadly Don started biting serving girls. Three nearly died from his attacks. By the age of 9 he was torturing little girls and animals for fun.

Don liked roasting small animals, like hares, alive (the little girls he liked to whip). He once carved up a stableful of horses so badly that 20 had to be put down.

Don was chasing a girl when he fell down stairs and gashed his head. His head swelled up. No one could cure him. So priests took the mummy of old St Diego, who'd been dead a hundred years, and popped it into bed with Don.

Bizarrely, his wound got better but he grew more unpredictable. He was a few pints short of a milk churn, had violent rages and attacked people. He tried to throw a servant out of a tower window. He made a shoemaker cut up a pair of boots and eat them.

He told a priest he wanted 'to kill a man' … and it was clear the man he wanted to kill was his own dad, King Philip. Philip had his son locked in the tower of Arévalo Castle.

Don Carlos had a fever and was sick non-stop. He poured iced water on the floor of his prison so that he could lie naked in it. Snow was brought in great barrels to cool him. For days he ate only fruit. Then he asked for a pie. A huge spicy pie was made for him and he ate it all. He washed it down with more than 10 litres of ice water. His sickness grew worse. When a priest came to pray for him Don threw up over the priest.

He died soon after. Murder?

King Philip gave his son everything he wanted in his prison, but the greedy prince stuffed himself with partridge livers washed down with iced water. This gave him a chill and he died. Not murdered but dead of his own greed.

Of course Philip's enemies said that he had ordered his son's murder.

He was perhaps the worst king England never had. Or was he? There is a legend that Elizabeth I was once courted by Ivan IV (1530–84) of Russia, better known as Ivan the Terrible. This was the man who, at the age of 13, threw a rival to his death and later murdered his own heir in a fit of temper. Two lucky escapes for Elizabeth and England then.

Elizabeth ascendant

'To err is human; to forgive, divine.'

Alexander Pope (1688–1744), English poet

Bloody Mary? Or Divine Mary ... according to some historians. They argue she was forgiving of treachery against herself. She only burned the people guilty of the greater offence – treason against God. Mere rebels were set free, like Edward Courtenay, who was told to make himself scarce with a trip to the Continent.

Elizabeth, of course, had also been spared. Now she had her turn on the throne she would prove far more ruthless in her elimination of opposition ... like father like daughter. Yet no one calls that pair of charmers Bloody Henry or Bloody Bess, do they?

The history mystery

Queen Elizabeth I was famous for NEVER getting married.* But people said she fell in love with the handsome Robert Dudley (1532–88).

Trouble was, handsome Rob was already married to Amy Robsart. Then Amy died.

The story went around that she had been murdered. Make up your own mind.

- In December 1559 Amy moved to Cumnor Place, three miles from Oxford. Rob stayed in London.

---

* In a rare moment of rebellion in 1566, Parliament told Elizabeth they'd refuse to raise taxes if she failed to take a husband. It was a game of bluff that Elizabeth won.

- Stories went around that Rob was trying to poison her. The poison didn't work.
- On 8 September 1560 she sent the servants off to Abingdon Fair. Why? Did she want to be alone or was she expecting a secret assignation?
- When the servants returned, they found her dead at the bottom of the stairs.

Did she throw herself down the stairs? Was she unhappy because Rob was flirting with the queen? Was it suicide?

Did she slip and fall? Some people say she was a sick woman. Was it an accident?

Or did Rob arrange to have her pushed? That's what his enemies said. Was it murder?

Another clue … Amy Dudley was buried at St Mary's, Oxford. Rob didn't go to the funeral.

Guilty or not? In fact the verdict of history is largely irrelevant. The gossip was enough to warn Elizabeth away from marrying him. Mud sticks.

Making progress

> 'If you think of paying court to the men in power, your eternal ruin is assured.'
>
> *Stendhal (1783–1842), French writer*

Elizabeth began the lifestyle that was to be a pattern throughout her life with the royal household travelling about the realm from manor to manor. The 'progress', as it was known, tended to stay long enough to devour the supplies of one district before moving on to find new pastures to ravage. With 300 carts required to supply hay and oats alone, there would have been enough to feed Henry VIII for a day.

To the locals, it must have seemed like a visitation of a biblical plague.

> 'In appearance the locusts were like horses prepared for battle: on their heads were what looked like crowns of gold; their faces were like human faces, their hair like women's hair.'
>
> *Revelation 9:7*

When Queen Liz and her entourage arrived at your home they expected …

- rich gifts – gold and jewels were best
- entertainments – music, plays and sports
- the best rooms for herself and her court

The honour was great … but the cost could be greater. And it wasn't just the aristocratic hosts that had to fork out. It was the ordinary people of the districts she visited. Their homes had to have a face-lift before Elizabeth set her regal eyes upon them.

A grammar school in Norwich paid out 9 shillings and 4 pence (two weeks' wages for a teacher) just to paint the door and clean up three loads of 'street muck' outside. The trembling headmaster gave a speech of welcome to Elizabeth (in Latin) and she let him kiss her hand.

Everywhere Elizabeth went her people spent their hard-earned money cleaning their towns and villages. She must have thought England was cleaner than Switzerland.

On that visit to Norwich the people of the city were given orders weeks before she arrived …

- Put fresh plaster on the walls of your hovel (just the side the queen will see).
- Clean up your outside toilets so the smell doesn't knock passing birds from the sky.
- Repair the paths outside your house, even though Liz won't be walking on them.
- Keep your cows off the streets – milk them in the fields or your yard.
- Sweep your chimneys.*

In addition, butchers who killed cattle inside the city had to take the waste outside and bury it. (Makes you wonder what they did with it before.) No cows, pigs or horses were to be kept in the castle ditch.

Did you know … thatch catch

Hosting Elizabeth had some disastrous and unforeseen consequences. One spectacular firework display caused the thatch of a peasant's cottage to catch alight. The humble home was destroyed. Elizabeth (uncharacteristically) paid for the place to be rebuilt.†

Why did Elizabeth make her people go to all this trouble? There were two conventional reasons … plus one that most history books don't mention:

* The fine for a chimney fire was 6 shillings and 8 pence.

† And hopefully the careless fireworks master got a rocket.

1 Elizabeth wanted her people to see her – she loved being cheered by her faithful subjects. She understood the value of her celebrity aura.

2 The plague came to London most summers and it was safer to travel round in the fresher air of the countryside.

3 Toilets. Toilets? You are probably asking yourself, 'What have toilets got to do with the queen going on a tour about the countryside?' (Even if you are not asking yourself this, you are going to be told.)

In Tudor England the great houses and palaces had little rooms known as 'jakes' set aside for ablutions. But the 'waste' from the jakes didn't get washed away. It fell down into a pit. With hundreds of people living in a palace, these pits soon filled up … and up … and up.

> 'My wife and I were married in a toilet – it was a marriage of convenience!'
>
> *Tommy Cooper (1921–84), English comedian*

The pits had to be opened, the ordure shovelled up and carted away. While this was going on it was not exactly rose-scented in your home. The smell could hang around for weeks. The solution was to move out while they were emptied. This process was known, charmingly, as a 'sweetening'. That's what the Tudor monarchs did. That's why they had three or four palaces and kept moving around.

Best of all, Elizabeth could move around to other people's houses and fill up *their* jakes. Then she could move on and leave the owners to clear up after her and her court.

Waste disposal of all sorts was a problem in the Elizabethan world. Even though they didn't understand the science of disease, they appreciated the health benefits of sweetly swept streets.

In 1563 each man in London was ordered to burn his rubbish three times a week to suppress the spread of disease. The mayor and council ordered …

> 'That the filthy dunghill lying in the highway near unto Finsbury Court be removed and carried away.'*

— THE ODDS-ON FAVOURITE —

> 'You are like my little dog; when people see you, they know I am nearby.'
>
> *Elizabeth I to 'favourite' Robert Dudley*

The Duke of Northumberland had paid for his plot to enthrone Lady Jane Grey with his life. His son, Robert Dudley, was sentenced to death too … then reprieved. He was in the Tower of London at the same time as Elizabeth.

Robert Dudley later became one of her greatest 'favourites' and probably came as close to marrying Elizabeth as anyone. So, of course, the legend arose that they had met in the Tower when they were both imprisoned there. Mills and Boon authors would love that image … their eyes met over a groaning rack, while their love burned hot as a branding iron … perhaps.†

---

* These days a football club called Arsenal play adjacent to Finsbury. Some people – usually jealous rivals – still complain about the rubbish they see there. The club has not been invited to take it elsewhere.

† It was dangerous to say that in Elizabeth's lifetime, mind you. An

Elizabeth was closely guarded with the express purpose of preventing any meetings with anti-Mary contacts. A meeting between the two is as likely as a meeting of a turkey with Santa's sleigh.

This favourite had as rich and varied a life as any Tudor gent …

Dudley was released by Mary so he could fight with her husband, Philip of Spain, in Flanders. Philip won that battle and had an original way of commemorating the victory, which was won on St Lawrence's Day, 1557. St Lawrence had been martyred on a red-hot gridiron, so Philip had a palace built near Madrid in the shape of a gridiron.*

Dudley was another of Elizabeth's favourites who refused to be married off to Mary, Queen of Scots. As a Puritan supporter he'd have negated Mary's Catholic threat … but it would probably have led to a marriage made in hell. He sympathized with Mary until the 1580s, then, like a weather vane on a wild winter's day, swung round and argued for her execution. He was such a favourite Elizabeth showered him with grants of land that made him one of the richest men in England.

He was another favourite who failed to marry Elizabeth. When Dudley's wife died in those mysterious circumstances in 1560 he was free to marry the queen. But suspicions of his being involved in his wife's death put a stop to that. A coroner's jury said her fall down stairs was 'accidental death' but the prudish public couldn't have a queen tainted by murder … which is odd. Elizabeth's father Henry VIII had

---

Essex man who said Queen Elizabeth had two children by Dudley was imprisoned for three years. *Hello!* magazine would not have flourished under such severe penalties for repeating royal gossip.

* Not a lot of people know that. In fact you could be the only person on your pub-quiz team to have that rare fact. Cherish it.

a lot of involvement in the judicial murder of two wives yet that didn't debar him from the throne. One law for a Tudor man, another for a Tudor woman.

> 'If Satan ever laughs, it must be at hypocrites; they are the greatest dupes he has; they serve him better than any others, and receive no wages.'
>
> *Charles Caleb Colton (1780–1832), English cleric*

Elizabeth couldn't have Dudley but, sure as God made little green frogs, she didn't want any other woman to have him. He stayed single for 18 years. When he eventually married Lettice Knollys in 1578 he was banned from court for the rest of his life. Hell hath no fury like Elizabeth scorned. Lettice was Elizabeth's first cousin once removed – removed from court when she upset the queen. Lettice led an interesting life.

Dudley was given top jobs. As soon as Elizabeth took the throne he was made Master of the Horse. That doesn't sound much but in fact it was the palace No. 3.* He commanded part of the English fleet against the Spanish Armada and he was the bright spark who invited Queen Elizabeth to visit her troops at Tilbury. That was to be one of the events in her life that made her a legend.

In the 1560s when Dutch Protestants began revolting against Spanish rule, Dudley went to help the Protestant cause and accepted the role of governor. As well as enraging Queen Elizabeth, the expedition ruined him financially.

After suffering an illness, probably stomach cancer, Dudley died in 1588 aged 56. Elizabeth was distraught at the loss and locked herself in her apartment for hours, if not

* And no facetious remarks, please, about it being stable employment.

days. She treasured the letter he had sent her a short while before his death, and she wrote on it: 'His Last letter'. She put it in her souvenir box. It was discovered there when she died 15 years later.

Elizabeth's love did not extend to Dudley's wife Lettice. The widow struggled to pay the debts the late Robert had incurred in the service of the queen. Elizabeth did nothing to help. Elizabeth's grandfather, Henry VII, had been notorious for his meanness with money.

Did you know ... Robert Dudley: serial killer?

Lettice Knollys had married Dudley's rival, the Earl of Essex, in 1560. She returned to court in 1565 but was too fond of flirting with Dudley so a jealous Elizabeth sent her packing.

Essex was sent to Ireland to quell uprisings in 1573. While he was away (the Catholic scandal-mongers said) Lettice and her illicit lover, Dudley, produced a daughter. When Essex was due to return home she aborted a second child, to destroy the evidence, as it were. Lettice prey? There was no proof of this but tongues wag as happily as dogs' tails where the mighty are concerned.

Dudley married Lettice after her husband Essex died in Dublin in 1576 of dysentery. There was a dysentery epidemic so it is unsurprising – an enquiry supported the diagnosis of 'natural causes'. But of course the rumours screamed, 'Poison. Poisoned by Dudley.' As Mark Twain said, 'Never let the truth get in the way of a good story.'

Lettice married Dudley in a quiet 7 a.m. ceremony when her two years of official mourning were completed. Elizabeth was spitting feathers when she heard of it. Five years later she still hadn't calmed down. There was a story that Lettice's daughter was a possible bride for Mary, Queen of Scots' son, James. Elizabeth said she'd rather give her crown to James than see him marry the child of that 'she-wolf' Lettice.

Dudley died suddenly in 1588 but Lettice's dramatic life was far from finished. In 1589 she married Sir Christopher Blount, a poor Catholic soldier 12 years younger. (So no two-year official mourning this time around.) It will come as no surprise that rumour had it she'd poisoned Dudley on his sick-bed because young buck Chris Blount was already her lover. Dudley, they whispered, was plotting to kill Lettice because of her affair so she simply got her retaliation in first.

Lettice's son, the young Earl of Essex, became Elizabeth's favourite and led a rebellion in 1601. Sir Christopher Blount had been a leading supporter of his stepson and followed young Essex to the block five weeks later.

Lettice went on to outlive her other children, as well as her childhood playmate Elizabeth by 30 years. She walked a mile a day till the end of her life and died peacefully in her chair on Christmas Day 1634 aged 91.

We'll never know if she forgave Elizabeth.

— THE SCARS —

Elizabeth had survived the power struggles while her siblings reigned. She also survived illnesses, including the dangerous smallpox when she was 30. Those who survived were often disfigured.

In Shakespeare's *Love's Labour's Lost*, the Princess of France's lady-in-waiting, Rosaline, makes a tart remark about the round pockmarks on Katharine's face … the result of smallpox:

> ROSALINE: O, that your face were not so full of Os!
> KATHARINE: A pox of that jest!

Later in the play these characters wear masks, which causes plot confusion among lovers.

There was a story that a noblewoman from Elizabeth's court took to wearing a mask to hide her smallpox-scarred face. Robert Dudley's sister, Mary (1532–86), came down with smallpox while attending Elizabeth. Her husband, Sir Henry Sidney, described her suffering …

> 'When I went to Newhaven I left her a full fair Lady in mine eye and when I returned I found her as foul a lady as the smallpox could make her. The scars ever since hath don and doth remain in her face, so as she lies like a night-raven in her house.'

A story said Mary only ever appeared in public in a mask. That's certainly not true but she DID become withdrawn and solitary. Mary caught the disease while nursing Elizabeth in 1562. And how did Elizabeth reward the loyalty of such a faithful servant? As befitted the daughter of Henry VIII, she 'rewarded' Mary with the sack. What else did you expect?

Mary and her husband died in desperate debt.

Elizabeth was given the 'Red Treatment', which seems to have involved wrapping her body in a red blanket.

Did you know … spot the connection

Most of the relatives of Henry VIII were infected with smallpox. They included …

- Margaret, Queen of Scots – sister
- Mary, Queen of Scots – great-niece
- Anne of Cleves – wife (infected before she married)
- Edward VI – son
- Elizabeth I – daughter

Whereas about 30 per cent of smallpox victims died from the disease, in this list only Edward died – of complications. But smallpox was more deadly for children so the survival rate for the royals was not unusual.

The smallpox didn't prove fatal as it did to many of her subjects. But it would affect her life.

Elizabeth whitened her skin, and hid her scars, with a mixture of egg, powdered eggshells, poppy seeds, white lead, borax and alum. The white lead was the lethal ingredient. It ate into her skin, so she had to apply more and more layers. It seeped into her blood and her hair began to thin, which obliged her to wear a huge spangled red wig.

For those of you who require a white face, covered in a paste that will fill up your smallpox scars, then there is no need to risk lead poisoning. There are alternative recipes for face-creams that will make you drop-dead gorgeous instead of drop-dead dead. Try this top tip from Sir Hugh Plat, *c.* 1602 …

Irresistible makeovers

> 'Wash the lard from a castrated pig in May-dew then take marshmallow roots, scraping off the outsides. Make thin slices of them and mix them. Set them to steep in a seething bath and scum it well till it be thoroughly clarified and it will turn glutinous. Apply to the face.'*

Tudor tooth-whitening would be disapproved of by the NICE people at National Institute for Health and Care Excellence. Tudor advice to rub the teeth with cuttlefish bone powder would be acceptable. Rinsing with white wine and 'spirit of vitriol' would *not*, because 'spirit of vitriol' is better known today as sulphuric acid. Not so nice.

When the tooth-whitening eroded the enamel on your teeth a cheap form of 'alternative' dentistry was performed by the local blacksmith.

But before we mock the ignorance of our ancestral superstitions, consider this beauty treatment to keep looking youthful …

> 'It involves mixing poo from a nightingale with rice bran and water which is then applied as a face mask.'†

---

* Or feed it to your husband if the first flush of romance has drained out of your marriage.

† The nightingales were fed on caterpillars that fed on plum trees, should you wish to replicate this. So much rarer than castrated pigs.

The baby-faced buyers are celebrities. The date not 1514 but 2014.

— POWDER PLOT AND PRISON —

Elizabeth became skilled at the art of survival in the regal jungle. She may not have worn a mask, but she was skilled at adopting different 'faces' depending on whom she was dealing with.

> 'For to win one hundred victories in one hundred battles is not the acme of skill. To subdue the enemy without fighting is the acme of skill.'
>
> *Sun Tzu (544–496 BC), Chinese military strategist*

Her cousin Mary, Queen of Scots, preferred a more direct, reckless approach when it came to dealing with problems.

> 'The best way out is always through.'
>
> *Robert Frost (1874–1963), American poet*

Mary was no luckier in love than Elizabeth.

- Husband no. 1, King Francis II of France, died in 1560 of an ear infection that led to an abscess in his brain.
- Her negotiations to marry Don Carlos – the mad heir to the Spanish throne, and rejected suitor of Elizabeth, came to nothing.*

---

* Not many people have been so busy not being king of places that didn't want them.

- Cousin Elizabeth promised to make Mary her heir on condition that she married Liz's favourite, Lord Dudley. The affronted Dudley refused to be a pawn in the game of thrones.
- A French poet called Chastelard was in love with Mary. He wanted to charm her with his songs so he hid under her bed. When hysterical Mary saw him there she screamed, the troubadour was dragged out and sentenced to death. Mary watched the execution as the poet sang out, 'I am dying for love of you, my most beautiful and cruel princess in the world.'* As auditions go it was X-factor to Axe-factor for the warbling wally.
- Mary married her English cousin Lord Darnley in 1565. This infuriated both the English and the Scots. The latter rebelled. Their consolation was that Mary refused to name the arrogant Darnley as the heir to her Scottish throne. He was frustrated and enraged. The marriage began to crack.
- Mary's favourite was the musician David Rizzio. He was rumoured to be father to the baby Mary was expecting. In 1566 Darnley had Rizzio murdered.

If life was dangerous in England then it was positively lethal for lovers of Mary, Queen of Scots.

Her revenge on hubby Darnley was only a few months in the gestation. Baby James was born, heir to the throne, and Darnley saw his ambitions disappearing over the Trossachs faster than a flying haggis. It was no secret that Mary was

* The truth is he probably cried it in French. She was fluent in the language, he was soon fluid from the neck.

getting rather too close to his replacement – the Earl of Bothwell.

Mary discussed divorce with her nobles. Darnley felt his life was under threat. Who can blame him when the lords said …

> 'It was thought most profitable that such a young fool and proud tyrant should not reign or bear rule over them; that he should be put off by one way or another; and whosoever should take the deed in hand or do it, they should defend.'
>
> *Confession of James Ormiston, a servant of the Earl of Bothwell*

It was a licence to kill.

The royal reject Darnley set off for his home in Glasgow. He was ill before he left Edinburgh … as usual, poison is suspected. Mary's first attempt on his life?

In January 1567 Mary persuaded Darnley to return to her loving arms. She visited him daily as he recovered from his illness. On the evening of 9 February 1567 she left his sickbed early to attend a wedding feast. It would prove a wonderful, and convenient, alibi. For in the early hours an explosion shook Darnley's house. Darnley was found dead in the garden … apparently suffocated.

Elizabeth gloated. As a 'faithful cousin' and 'affectionate friend' she wrote to Mary to pass on the gossip.

> 'I should tell you what all the world is thinking. Men say that, instead of seizing the murderers, you are looking through your fingers while they escape.'

For sheer hypocrisy Elizabeth couldn't be matched when she threw up her hands in horror and added …

> 'I beg you to believe that I would not harbour such a thought.'

Yes, right, Elizabeth, we believe you.

Bothwell was suspected of the murder but cleared for lack of evidence. In April 1567 he 'celebrated' by kidnapping Mary. He engineered a quickie divorce from his first wife and married the Queen of Scots.

Yet again she was soon disappointed in love. She was jinxed and never got to enjoy her power. Let's hope she enjoyed her games of golf better.*

> 'As you walk down the fairway of life you must smell the roses, for you only get to play one round.'
>
> *Ben Hogan (1912–97), American golfer*

The marriage shocked the Scots so much that Bothwell was driven into exile† and Mary was imprisoned. She escaped a year later and fled to England, expecting Elizabeth to support her return to the Scottish throne.

Elizabeth welcomed her as the spider welcomes the fly – or as a modern UKIP voter welcomes an asylum seeker. Mary was held prisoner while an English commission looked into the murder of Darnley. A casket of letters from Mary to murderer Bothwell were produced. Mary said they were forgeries.‡

---

* Mary was reputedly the first woman to play golf in Scotland. She caused a scandal when she was seen playing the game at St Andrews within days of Darnley's murder.

† He went to Denmark but was imprisoned, became insane and died in 1578.

‡ Historians have argued endlessly about the Casket Letters. The truth is, the authenticity doesn't matter. They didn't convict Mary anyway. Her son James destroyed the originals.

Mary was neither convicted nor cleared. She was simply kept locked away in a series of Elizabeth's castles while Elizabeth decided what to do with her dangerous cousin.

That decision took a mere 19 years. Elizabeth was nothing if not patient.

> 'I'm extraordinarily patient provided I get my own way in the end.'
>
> *Margaret Thatcher (1925–2013), British Prime Minister*

BRIEF TIMELINE – THE YOUNG QUEEN

1560 The Virgin Queen has a 'favourite' – Lord Robert Dudley. When Dudley's wife dies from a mysterious fall down stairs the queen is suspected of having a hand in it.*

Suitor Erik of Sweden abandons his marriage proposals after his trip to England is aborted on the death of his father.

1561 When the King of France dies, Mary, Queen of Scots, returns to rule Scotland. But she's a Catholic – in her absence Scotland has turned determinedly Protestant. Tense. And not a comfortable neighbour for Elizabeth.

1562 Elizabeth falls ill with smallpox and England panics because there is no obvious heir. She recovers. Captain John Hawkins sets off to break

---

* Not a personal hand in the back of Amy Dudley, you understand. A metaphorical hand.

the Spanish trade monopoly in the Atlantic. It'll upset them – again.

1563 Now Hawkins discovers the massive profits to be made from selling African slaves to the Americas. The Spanish confiscate half his fleet and declare him a pirate, but he still makes a fortune.

1564 A bard day in Stratford when William Shakespeare is born and survives a plague epidemic in the town. Phew.

Favourite Dudley promoted by Elizabeth to be Earl of Leicester. Elizabeth suggests Dudley marry Mary, Queen of Scots, but …

1565 … he's not keen and, anyway, Mary marries her cousin Henry Lord Darnley and …

1567 … Darnley is murdered. Bothwell is certainly the man who murdered Darnley. Mary, Queen of Scots, marries Bothwell. Shock. Scandal. She is forced to abdicate and …

1568 … flees to England where Elizabeth promptly locks her away.

England is nearly bankrupt so Elizabeth's ministers simply seize Spanish treasure ships when they arrive in Plymouth and Southampton. Spanish upset – yet again.

1569 Northern lords rebel and march south to set Mary free from her imprisonment. But they lose their nerve and flee before they meet Elizabeth's forces. Still it's a warning of the danger of a living Mary. She's a focus for Catholic disaffection.

Martyred Margaret

> 'You can chain me, you can torture me, you can even destroy this body, but you will never imprison my mind.'
>
> *Mahatma Gandhi (1869–1948), Indian nationalist*

The treatment of Margaret Clitheroe (1553–86) is probably a good guide to the paranoia of Elizabeth's enforcers.

The consequences are probably the most dramatic event never to be recorded by historians.*

Margaret Clitheroe, the Pearl of York,† died horribly in 1586 as the tensions with Spain were ratcheted up. Margaret's crime? None. Or maybe you can join the jury to decide. Look at the facts …

1 Margaret was two years old when Catholic Queen Mary died and Protestant Elizabeth came to the throne. On the religious roundabout the family had to switch religions yet again or hide their Catholicism. They stayed Catholic. Margaret's fate was sealed at the age of two.

---

* Oh, all right, that is enigmatic and teasing. But be patient and you'll see what I mean.

† You didn't get a lot of oysters in York producing pearls. But the name 'Margaret' means 'Pearl'. It's a play on words. Not a very subtle one. Margaret's mum must have been the Mother of Pearl then?

2 In 1571 Margaret (aged fifteen) married butcher John Clitheroe of the Shambles in York* and they had three children. John, her husband, was a Protestant but had a brother who went to train as a Catholic priest in Reims. A death sentence for the butcher's brother if he were caught.†

3 Margaret's husband was responsible for reporting Catholic worshippers in the parish. Awkward. She was first imprisoned in 1577 for skipping church. Two more terms in jail at York Castle followed – the second lasted 20 months. Did jail teach her to be a conforming Protestant? No. Did it teach her to read? Yes, actually.

4 By 1583 five priests had been executed at Knavesmire in York – now the racecourse. Margaret went on recklessly holding Catholic masses in her home and cut a hole into the adjoining house so her guest priest could escape when there was a raid by the religious police.

5 Mrs Clitheroe was eventually caught when her frightened young son revealed the secret chapel-room to the authorities. She was taken to court and asked to plead guilty or not guilty. But there was a catch.

---

* The 'Shambles' derived its name from the butcher shops that once filled its cobbles with guts. 'Shambles' is a corruption of the Anglo-Saxon 'fleshammels' or 'flesh-shelves'. Even 130 years ago there were still 25 independent butchers there. Today there are none. Why have they closed? There asda be some lidl clue to their demise. Margaret's house (a martyr's shrine) can still be seen there.

† I could say the steaks were high. But I'd never stoop so low.

6 She was faced with an impossible choice:

(a) Plead 'guilty' – she would be executed and her children would be disinherited

(b) Plead 'not guilty' – her children and servants would be tortured till they betrayed her

7 She refused to plead. The authorities were wise to that trick.

> 'Such felons as stand mute, and speak not at their arraignment, are pressed to death by huge weights laid upon a board that lieth over their breast, and a sharp stone under their backs. And these that held their peace, thereby to save their goods unto their wives and children, which, if they were condemned, should be confiscated to the prince.'
>
> *William Harrison*

8 They would place weights on her body and 'press' her until the pain was so great she WOULD plead one way or another. Margaret shrugged and said, 'God be thanked, I am not worthy of so good a death as this.'

9 Margaret was taken to the bridge over the River Ouse so a large number of York residents could watch and learn a lesson. Then the authorities hit a snag. No one wanted the job of pressing the woman to death. Eventually three beggars were persuaded to take on the grim task. Cruelty, the psychiatrist says, damages the inflictor too …

> 'The healthy man does not torture others – generally it is the tortured who turn into torturers.'
>
> *Carl Jung*

10 The woman was stretched out on the ground with a sharp rock under her back and a door was placed over her. Stones were placed on top of the door. Despite the increasing pain she still refused to plead. Eventually her bones were broken and she died within 15 minutes.*

Margaret is remembered in The Shambles where she lived. But her death poses questions … and that most dramatic event never to be recorded by historians that I mentioned.

The moral maze (1)

> 'Anything worth dying for … is certainly worth living for.' *Joseph Heller, 'Catch-22'*

Margaret Clitheroe chose her death. She has become a martyr and her persecutors are reviled. But reports say she was pregnant at the time – which drops a minefield into the maze. Did the Protestants murder an innocent unborn? And did Margaret knowingly allow an innocent foetus to die?

The moral maze (2)

> 'There are causes worth dying for, but none worth killing for.' *Albert Camus (1913–60), French author*

The pressing of Margaret was politically inept. Women were often sentenced to death for crimes such as infanticide, and even highway robbery, but a majority were pardoned. So did

---

* Should you be interested, the weight needed to crush a martyr is between 7 and 8 hundredweight or 350 to 400 kilos.

Margaret Clitheroe's horrific death *inspire* Catholic devotion rather than deter it?

Historians will (probably) never know the truth. But a 15-year-old Protestant boy from York was *likely* to have witnessed the horrific treatment of Margaret.

We know that the boy definitely converted to Catholicism. When he grew up he sought to end such Protestant atrocities by replacing the monarch with someone who had Catholic sympathies. He planned (but failed) to do it violently. Did he witness Margaret's execution? Did THAT turn his thoughts to terrorism? Was he justified?

The York teen's name was Guy Fawkes. Terrorist. Or fighter for justice?

Did you know … pressing

… was not used for only religious crimes. Any refusal to plead could end up with you being pressed to death … especially if you lived in York.

Walter Calverly wasted his family fortune on drink. In a drunken frenzy, he stabbed his two eldest children, William (four years) and Walter (18 months). He turned on his wife, and stabbed her but not fatally. He then rode off to a nurse's cottage where a third young son, Henry, was being cared for. He planned to kill him too, but he was apprehended on the road. He was tried at York but refused to plead. His punishment was to be pressed to death in York Castle.

The story was dramatized as *A Yorkshire Tragedy – not so new as lamentable and true* in 1608, and advertised as 'written by W. Shakespeare'. But it wasn't. Who wrote it? Who knows? Probably Thomas Middleton … but he's dead, so he's not confirming or denying it.

– THE FORGOTTEN KILLER –

The tortures and executions were spectacular. But simply being incarcerated in a place like the Tower could be deadly in itself.

If the damp, unheated cells didn't get you then the water might. For foul water could be as deadly poisonous as prussic acid. Slower-acting but a filthier fate.

DANGEROUS DAYS DEATH IV

TYPHOID

Salmonella typhi is the bacteria that causes typhoid. Another disease that's passed by hand-to-mouth transmission of other people's faeces.

It starts with a week of fever, coughing and generally feeling off-colour. By the second week the fever is really high, 40 °C+, almost combustible, and you can do nothing but lie in bed completely prostrate. Delirious, with red spots on your tummy, you enter the third week of illness for the start of the diarrhoea. Classically green, like pea soup, you pass so much each day that dehydration occurs.

Low on fluids and your heart weakened by the infection, your bowel bursts, peritonitis develops, followed by septicaemia as the infection spreads to the blood. Exhausted and with all your major organs shutting down, you die.

Dr Peter Fox

DAVID RIZZIO: THE SLICED SINGER 1565

'I am in blood
Stepp'd in so far that, should I wade no more,
Returning were as tedious as go o'er.'

Macbeth, *William Shakespeare*

Mary, Queen of Scots' life was as steeped in murder as Agatha Christie's. David Rizzio's death was a crime story stained with blood and tears.

David was a talented singer and a nice lad. Reports say he was an ugly little man, full of his own importance, with an expensive taste in clothes. But his voice was his fortune.

His big break in showbiz came when he sought a position in Mary, Queen of Scots' court. He only had to perform twice for the queen and she was hooked. She made him one of her *valets de chambre* (gentlemen of the privy chamber).

But Davy was more than a mere musician. The queen came to trust him and turned to him for counsel. In 1565 Rizzio encouraged the marriage of the queen to Henry Stewart, Lord Darnley. Rather like Joseph of the Technicolor Dreamcoat fame, he attracted the resentment of her senior advisors. They couldn't take a razor to his vocal cords – too obvious. So they tried something more subtle – in the way running someone over with a Routemaster bus is more subtle than running them over with a steamroller.

The courtiers played on Darnley's insecurities and hinted that Mary was having a 'relationship' with Rizzio.* When

* Darnley was not the brightest jewel in the royal crown. He was already having hissy fits because Mary made him her husband but refused to give him the title of 'King'.

Mary became pregnant, rumours spread that the baby was Rizzio's. (No paternity tests in the Elizabethan world to clear his name.)

> 'Woe is me for you when Davy's son shall be King of England.'
>
> *Scottish Lord Randolph to English Earl of Leicester*

Randolph was thinking ahead to the death of Elizabeth I and the likelihood that Mary's child would inherit the English throne. The infant, the future James VI and I, DID become King of England. But he was certainly the child of Darnley. The rumours were absurd ... but believed.

> 'Things least to be believed are most preferred.'
>
> *John Clare (1793–1864), English poet*

Darnley and the lords plotted Rizzio's murder ... in Mary's presence, just to make their message quite clear. That message would be writ in blood. Lots of it. The queen was at supper in the little room adjoining her bedchamber at Holyroodhouse. Suddenly Darnley marched in, sat down beside Mary, and put his arm around her waist. He chatted with a frenzied friendliness, then the figure of Patrick, Lord Ruthven, appeared in the doorway, deathly pale and wearing full armour. He must have looked like the ghost of Hamlet's father as he intoned ...

> 'May it please your majesty to let yonder man Davie come forth of your presence, for he has been overlong here!'

The short answer could have been 'No'. The long answer perhaps, 'You must be joking. Push off.'

But Mary was struck dumb. The queen rose to her feet in alarm. A terrified Rizzio darted behind her, clinging to the pleats of her gown as if that would do him any good. He wailed:

> 'Justice! Justice! Save my life, madame, save me!'*

The queen couldn't help because Andrew Kerr of Fawdonside held his pistol to her side, while George Douglas (Darnley's uncle) snatched Darnley's dagger from his belt and stabbed Rizzio. According to Mary's own memoir, this first blow was struck over her shoulder.

The murderers dragged Rizzio from the room and hewed him to death. Darnley ordered that the body, with 56 stab wounds, be flung down the staircase, and thrown across a casket where the porter's servant stripped him of his fine clothes.† They would need a good wash and a lot of darning to restore them, of course.

Weeping Mary asked over and over again what had happened to him. Hours later one of her ladies brought her the news that Rizzio was dead.

Mary, Queen of Scots, dried her eyes and murmured ominously …

> 'No more tears now, I will think upon revenge.'

Death followed Mary so closely it trod on the hem of her dress. The Grim Reaper must have been chafing his skeletal hands like cockroach wings when he heard that.

---

* An odd thing to cry. As he was being accused of naughty goings on with his royal mistress the savage stabbers could have shrugged and said, 'Justice, mate? This is it.'

† If 50 stab wounds looks like malice, 56 looks like someone lost control. Julius Caesar was stabbed a mere 23 times … though the result was the same. Do you ever wonder who has the job of counting stab wounds?

GALLEONS AND GALES

BRIEF TIMELINE – THE DANGER YEARS

1570 Around 450 Catholic rebels executed for the Northern rebellion. The queen is excommunicated by the pope who wants to encourage the rebels. One rich Catholic, John Felton, posts the pope's message on his door. Is Elizabeth amused? Hah! She has Felton tortured and executed.

1571 Now it's the Italian Ridolphi plot aiming to murder Elizabeth and put cousin Mary on the throne.

1572 Francis Drake starts attacking Spanish treasure ships. He's the first Englishman to see the Pacific. He returns with treasures but only 31 of the 73 crew who set sail survive. Expensive riches.

1575 Elizabeth progresses around the Midlands. At Kenilworth Robert Dudley tries to impress with poetry and plays, banquets and bear-baiting, fireworks and hunting. He pops the question … but the answer is 'No'.

1575 Now Francis Drake sets off to sail around the world.

1578 Elizabeth considers marriage to French Duke of Anjou … a Catholic. Protestant protestor, James Stubbs, has his hand cut off for daring to object. Leicester marries Lettice Knollys in secret. The queen sobs.

1579 The town of Norwich is proud to be honoured by a royal visit. The royal baggage train brings plague to the city and leaves it ravaged. 'Pride goeth before destruction, and an haughty spirit before a fall,' as King James's Bible will have it in 25 years' time.

— THE NORTHERN REPRISALS 1570 —

'Fear follows crime and is its punishment.' *Voltaire*

There is a brief, but misleading, version of this slice of history. It says that the Dukes of Northumberland and Westmorland were Catholics and wanted to put Mary, Queen of Scots, on the throne. But nothing is ever that simple.

The truth is the Dukes of Northumberland had been like kings of Northern England till Henry VIII took away their power. They wanted that power back. Wouldn't you?

Elizabeth's spies told her about the Northern Rebellion fomenting. She wrote to her lords commanding them to appear before her at her palace in Richmond.

Would you go? Not if you had a brain cell in your head and wanted to keep it there. Northumberland didn't dare ignore the majestic missive so he came up with an original reply. He said that, while he would dearly love to answer the summons, he was unable to attend as he was simply too busy at the moment.

Elizabeth wrote to Westmorland and was more forceful. Come, or else. Westmorland came up with a rather better excuse. He claimed he daren't come to London because he had enemies there. He would have to bring an army for protection and the queen wouldn't like that, would she? There is a subtle threat in there. Perhaps some other time, he suggested.

The queen's army, led by the Earl of Sussex, marched up to York … then stopped. The Northern dukes marched south towards them. They reached Durham – 75 miles north of their enemies. With no soldiers to attack, the Catholic rebels turned on the hated Protestant cathedral at Durham.

They destroyed the Protestant tables where services were held and the Protestant prayer books. But those Protestant tables were about to be turned.

The rebels marched inland to Barnard Castle, where the defenders began to desert and join the attacking army – the Catholic cause was clearly popular in the region. Since the gates were barred, the Barnard Castle deserters had to jump over the walls. The castle commander, Sir George Bowes, wrote a report …

> 'We were besieged by the rebels and were short of bread and water. I found people in the castle were in continual mutinies, seeking to betray the castle or leap the walls and run to the rebels. In one day the castle lost 226 soldiers, though 35 of these broke their necks, legs or arms in leaping.'*

---

* You can almost hear him adding mentally, 'Disloyal gits. Serves them right.'

In the end, he had to surrender.

The Northern rebels now held most of County Durham. But they hadn't captured the castles at Newcastle, Carlisle or Berwick – where no one jumped over the walls to greet them.

No other Northern lords joined them and no army arrived from Catholic friends in Spain. Elizabeth's forces finally began to move North to attack.

Lord Westmorland and Lord Northumberland did what any sensible rebel would do – they ran away.

The queen's forces murdered and looted their way North and wiped out any remaining rebel forces. Then they started punishing any rebels they could catch. Of 917 County Durham rebels captured, 228 were executed – about one in three.

There were 19 'gentlemen' among the 917 rebels captured. Here's an interesting thing. How many of the 19 'gentlemen' rebels were executed? You guessed it. Not one.

Of these gentlemen, 11 were sent into exile and 8 were pardoned. Not one was hanged. This wasn't a peasant revolt – this was a revolt of the lords. Yet when it came to punishments the gentlemen got away with it and the poor suffered.

One of the queen's spies, Sir Thomas Gargrave, wrote to his master, William Cecil, and said …

> 'The common people are saying that the poor are ruined or executed but the gentlemen and the rich escape.'

William Cecil was made Lord Burghley, so persecuting the poor was clearly a good career move.

One of the supporters of the Northern rebellion was the Duke of Norfolk, Britain's wealthiest landowner. When the revolt failed, Norfolk confessed and grovelled for his life. He was sent to the Tower of London for nine months.

– ROTTEN RIDOLPHI 1571 –

'Careless shepherd make excellent dinner for wolf.'

Earl Derr Biggers (1884–1933), American novelist

Lord Burghley became Elizabeth's master spy. He had to virtually invent the art of espionage from scratch. An early success came with the unravelling of the Ridolphi plot.

Allegedly it was a scheme that combined all the usual suspects – the pope, Mary, Queen of Scots, and Philip II of Spain. Ridolphi was a banker from Florence and he was coordinating the plan to invade with a Catholic army and march on London.

The Duke of Norfolk was given the task of seizing Queen Elizabeth. The 35-year-old Norfolk had been arrested in 1569 because he had plotted to marry Mary, Queen of Scots.* Those nine months' imprisonment in the Tower had taught him nothing. On his release he was plotting again. But of course Lord Burghley had the young lame-brain watched. Norfolk doesn't seem to have suspected he was a suspect … If you see what I mean. Plot tip 1 … if at first you don't succeed – give up.

Roberto di Ridolphi travelled Europe, making money and pulling together the strands of the plot. His problem was his inability to keep his mouth shut. He simply involved too many people and eventually one of them wrote a warning to Elizabeth. Plot tip 2 … careless talk costs lives, probably your own.

* Don't imagine this was a romantic defiance of danger. Norfolk was miffed because he felt Elizabeth undervalued him. Aiming to marry Mary was the act of a big spoilt kid.

Ridolphi's messenger was intercepted at Dover, compromising letters were discovered and the messenger sang like a canary when a little torture was applied. Ridolphi himself was on the continent at the time and wisely chose never to return to England. The scapegoat was Norfolk, who was executed in 1572.

Elizabeth wasn't persecuting Catholics because of paranoia. They really *were* out to get her. Ridolphi didn't want to depose Elizabeth and lock her away. He wanted her murdered.

> 'People say I am ruthless. I am not ruthless. And if I find the man who is calling me ruthless, I shall destroy him.'
>
> *Robert Kennedy (1925–68), US politician**

— THE TROUBLE WITH SPYING —

> SCARAMANGA: The English don't consider it sporting to kill in cold blood, do they?
>
> JAMES BOND: Don't count on that.
>
> *Ian Fleming (1908–64), English author* The Man with the Golden Gun

Burghley defended Elizabeth with his spy network. But it was a new profession and he had to use ingenuity to come up with original tactics. Could YOU have done it? Have a look at these real case histories …

---

* Who, unlike Elizabeth, was the victim of a successful assassination. Maybe he wasn't ruthless enough.

Dealing with the enemy

John Story was a Catholic and worked hard for Queen Mary I. When Mary died and Elizabeth came to the throne, Story escaped to Holland where he made a nuisance of himself. He began searching English ships and taking away any Protestant books the English wanted to smuggle into Holland. How would you stop him?

Solution: Spy-master Burghley sent an English ship to Holland full of Protestant books. A fake 'informer' let Story know the books were there. It was the cheese in the mousetrap. He stepped on board to impound them. The English crew kidnapped him and took him back to England for the usual treatment.*

Carrying secret messages (1)

James Painter worked for the English spy service. His task was to carry messages from Paris to London and bring back the replies without being caught. There was always a chance that the mail would be stolen and read by an enemy. How did James Painter keep his messages secret?

Solution: The messages were remembered by Painter and he carried them in his head. It is believed that Painter had a special memory method that he used to carry complicated messages … for your eyes only.

Carrying secret messages (2)

Codes can be broken, of course. If you were worried that the enemy might have a copy of your code then you had to

---

* If he were stretched on the rack would he become a Tall Story? Just wondering.

find another way to write a message. The answer was to use invisible ink. The paper looks harmless enough in normal light but if it is heated (or dipped in a chemical) then the secret message shows through. What do you use for invisible ink?

Solution: Urine. Milk could be used but didn't usually work so well as urine. Onion juice and orange juice were also used. More tasteful than pee.

Catching enemy messengers

A Spanish dentist was travelling through England. Elizabeth's spies suspected that he was carrying secret messages from Spanish Catholics to English Catholics. Searches of his dental equipment revealed secret letters. What would you, as a spy-catcher, do next?

Solution: Once they had found his hiding place the English spy-catchers decided it would be best to let him go on carrying messages because they could follow and uncover the English traitors he was working with.* The Spanish dentist could die another day.

– A PLETHORA OF PLOTS –

> 'There are more than two hundred men of all ages who, at the instigation of the Jesuits, conspire to kill me.'
>
> *Elizabeth I, letter to French ambassador (1583)*

---

* In fact the dentist hid letters in a secret compartment in a mirror. A messenger called Bisley had messages sewn into his buttons.

Pope Pius V excommunicated Elizabeth in 1570. His bull proclaimed her a heretic, making her a legitimate target for Catholic assassins.

> 'Elizabeth, the pretended queen of England and the servant of crime is deprived of her pretended title to the crown. We charge and command all the nobles and subjects that they do not dare obey her orders, mandates and laws.'
>
> Regnans in Excelsis, *papal bull (1570)*

In other words, 'Kill her and God will forgive you … it's not murder because she's a non-person.'

> 'One kills a man, one is an assassin; one kills millions, one is a conqueror; one kills everybody, one is a god.'
>
> *Jean Rostand (1894–1977), French philosopher*

Sir Francis Walsingham, Lord Burghley and their spies were Elizabeth's vital secret army – a first line of defence that would uncover plots before they flared up. And their efforts were rewarded.

The most bizarre plots were those involving witchcraft:

- Wax replicas of the queen and two of her councillors were found in the house of a Catholic priest. He meant to use them to end her life by black magic.
- One of Elizabeth's chamber ladies was accused of trying 'by witchcraft' to discover Elizabeth's life span; from there it was but a small step to shortening it.

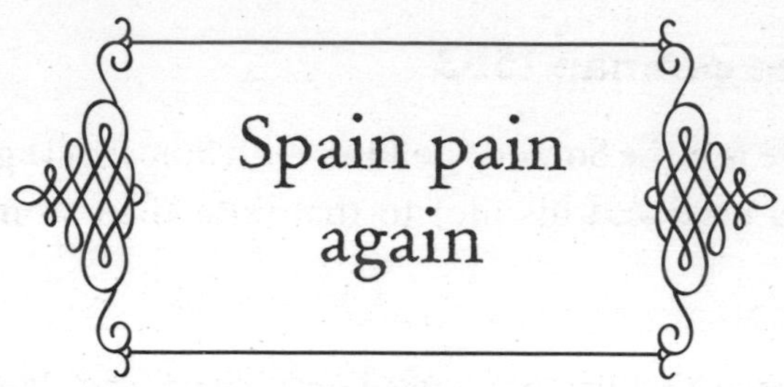

Spain pain again

In 1583 there were two attempts to overthrow Elizabeth. First came the Throckmorton Plot. The chief plotter was called Throckmorton … you probably guessed that. Sir Francis of that name was first cousin to Elizabeth's principal lady-in-waiting. Always handy to have friends in high places.

The plot was predictable and straightforward.

- Assassinate Elizabeth.
- Time it to coincide with an invasion led by Henry I, Duke of Guise.
- A simultaneous rising of English Catholics backed by the pope and Spanish gold.
- Place Mary, Queen of Scots, on the English throne.*

Spymaster Sir Francis Walsingham's agents heard of the plot and found incriminating evidence in Throckmorton's house. He denied it. He was tortured. He admitted it. He was executed.

Throckmorton's achievement was a negative one. Mary, Queen of Scots, was placed under still closer guard.

* And you can see the flaw. If Spanish cash has put her on the throne then Philip will want to share her power. England would be a Spanish colony.

The lone gunman 1583

Then there was the Somerville Plot. John Somerville gave his name (his neck and his life) to that little affair. Somerville said …

> 'I want to see Elizabeth's head on a pole, for she is a serpent and a viper.'

Impolite and impolitic. He was a bit of a snake in the grass himself. His method was quite straightforward: he'd take a pistol and shoot her. Admirable in its simplicity. He was intercepted and arrested.

He committed suicide by hanging himself in the Tower of London before the official death sentence could be carried out.

Parliamentary Parry plotter 1584

> 'We are only falsehood, duplicity, contradiction; we both conceal and disguise ourselves from ourselves.'
>
> *Blaise Pascal (1623–62), French mathematician, inventor, writer*

If 1583 was a bad year then 1584 wasn't turning out much better. Elizabeth I escaped death again and the would-be assassin was Dr William Parry, a Welsh MP.

Parry was a true ingrate. In 1580 he had killed one of his creditors in a violent quarrel and was sentenced to death. Good Queen Bess pardoned him and in 1584 made him a Member of Parliament.

Yet he repaid her by hiding in the garden at Richmond Palace with a pistol …

How could he fail? He had the pistol … or a knife, depending which version you believe … but he simply didn't have the bottle. Elizabeth's armour was her sheer force of personality. A report said Parry was …

> 'So daunted with the majesty of her presence in which he saw the image of her father, King Henry VIII …'

He could not bring himself to murder the queen.

His motives appear confused. He worked as a spy, so his story was that he was feigning being a regicide 'in order to infiltrate papist circles'.

Ingenious. 'I am pretending to be an assassin so I can get the real assassins to come out of the woodwork.'

The pope believed Parry to be a loyal Catholic assassin. Elizabeth's judges agreed. Parry was sentenced to death and ended his life on the gallows at Westminster. Again this plot led to a tightening of anti-Catholic laws. A new law ordered all seminary priests to leave England within 40 days or suffer the penalty for high treason.

Yet Elizabeth continued to allow Catholics in to her court and to walk freely among her subjects. That famous Englishman, God, would shield her. She told a group of foreign envoys…

> 'He who is on high has defended me until this hour, and will keep me still, for in Him I do trust.'

And God didn't let her down.

– MARY, QUEEN OF CHOPS –

Elizabeth's cousin, Mary, Queen of Scots, was a problem – a running sore as deep and incurable as Henry VIII's leg ulcer. As long as she lived she'd be the focus of the dissatisfied, the disgruntled and the downright devious. While she remained locked in one of Elizabeth's castles, there would always be some romantic dreamer who believed he could ride a white charger and rescue the damsel in distress. In their fairy-tale minds, Elizabeth was the wicked witch.

Throughout her 18 years in Elizabeth's castles, Mary was watched by spies. It would only take one proven plot to seal her death warrant. Mary knew that, yet still encouraged the white knights. White knights like Antony Babington.

The Babington bungle

> 'I have learned to hate all traitors, and there is no disease that I spit on more than treachery.'
>
> *Aeschylus (524–455 BC), Greek tragedian*

The 1586 plot was delightfully simple (if a little familiar):

1 Organize an invasion of Catholic armies from France, Spain, Italy and Scotland. Have English Catholics ready to fight with them as soon as they land.

2 Release Mary, Queen of Scots, from prison so she can be a new Catholic Queen of England. After all, she is Elizabeth's cousin and has a claim to the throne … when Elizabeth is dead. So …

3 Assassinate Queen Elizabeth. A man called John 'How-appropriate-is-my-surname' Savage has vowed to kill her and six 'gentlemen' have agreed to help.

One of the plotters was a young man called Antony Babington. The plot became named after him even though he wasn't the most important plotter.*

You will notice that all the plots against Elizabeth failed. Partly because of her efficient spy system but also because the plotters were not blessed with the brains of a wren.

Birdbrain Babington wrote to Mary, Queen of Scots, in secret and asked, 'Will you write to give your approval for our plot?' He handed the letter to a servant to deliver. He had no inkling that his 'servant' was a spy for Elizabeth.

The servant took it to Sir Francis Walsingham (1532–90), principal secretary to Queen Elizabeth but more popularly remembered as her 'spy-master'.

Walsingham could have destroyed it and scotched the plot – no pun intended. He was too crafty for that. He knew that Mary had a secret delivery of letters carried in a beer barrel. But as Walsingham said, 'She doesn't know that we know.'

Did you know … messages in a barrel

Walsingham placed double-agent Gilbert Gifford and code-breaker Thomas Phelippes inside Chartley Hall where Queen Mary was imprisoned.† Gifford managed the Walsingham plan, which was worthy of a World War Two SAS operation. The messages were secreted in a beer-barrel cork. The replies, using the same device, were then intercepted by Phelippes, decoded and the transcription sent to Walsingham. The originals were passed on to the plotters, who suspected nothing.

---

* Rather like the gunpowder plot almost 20 years later. That was named after Guy Fawkes, who was really just one lesser cog in the death machine.

† Gilbert Gifford had been a Catholic priest so was above suspicion. He had defected to Walsingham's spy-catchers in 1585. What's not to trust … until the knife is plunged in your back? *Et tu*, backstabber.

Mary received the Babington letter, read of the plot and her indiscreet reply sealed her fate. She told them, 'Assassinate Elizabeth, if that's necessary for my release.'

Walsingham must have grinned with grim glee as he read Mary's reply. This is what Elizabeth's protectors had been waiting for – waiting for 16 years. The order went out to arrest the plotters.

The treacherous servant simply invited the main plotters to his house for dinner. During the meal Babington suddenly got to his feet and tried to flee. He was captured, tortured, then interviewed again. Walsingham thoughtfully wrote a confession for Babington to sign. Both Babington and Ballard were executed in September 1586.

Babington was hanged, drawn and quartered. For those not familiar with this sadistic capital punishment, an eye-witness can enlighten you …

> 'The greatest and most grievous punishment used in England for such as offend against the State is drawing from the prison to the place of execution upon an hurdle or sled, where they are hanged till they be half dead, and then taken down, and quartered alive; after that, their members and bowels are cut from their bodies, and thrown into a fire, provided near hand and within their own sight, even for the same purpose.'
>
> *William Harrison*

Such was the public outcry at the horror of Babington's execution that Queen Elizabeth changed the order. Subsequent plotters would be allowed to hang until dead before being disembowelled.

Such a consolation, I'm sure you will agree.

The Fotheringhay Farce

In October 1586 Queen Mary was given a preposterous trial at Fotheringhay Castle in Northamptonshire. She was not allowed legal counsel, or permitted to see the evidence against her, or to provide witnesses for the defence.* Portions of spy Phelippes' letter translations were read at the trial. They damned her.

A good defence lawyer would have pointed out that, as the Scottish queen, she could hardly be convicted of treason against England – a foreign country. One of the 46 English lords on the jury voted not guilty. Brave man.

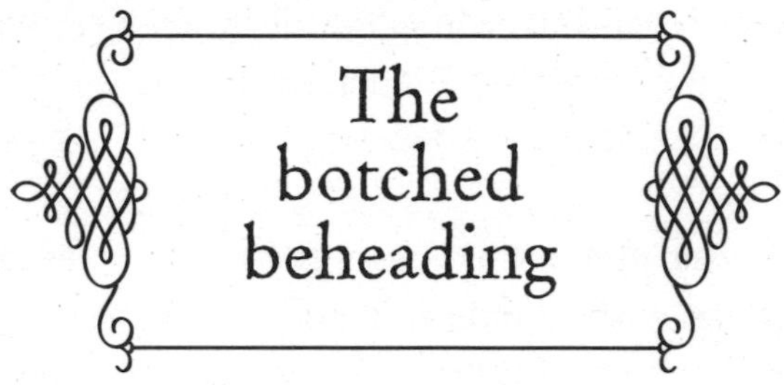

> 'Her prayers being ended, the executioners, kneeling, desired her Grace to forgive them her death: who answered, 'I forgive you with all my heart, for now, I hope, you shall make an end of all my troubles.'
>
> *Robert Wynkfield, witness to execution of Mary, Queen of Scots*

Elizabeth sent a message to Mary's jailer, Sir Amias Paulet (1532–88), suggesting it would be better if Mary were quietly

---

* Witnesses for the defence may have been interesting, don't you think? 'Yes, she arranged the murder of her husband 20 years ago, but she hasn't murdered anyone since she's been locked away in England. And she is very good at golf. Beheading would ruin her handicap.'

murdered. She could then deny responsibility quite neatly – even attract sympathy for a tragic loss of her beloved cousin. But Sir Amias was horrified and refused.

A formal execution had to go ahead. Elizabeth signed the order, dispatched a messenger with it … and then appeared to change her mind. She was still trying to say, 'I never wanted dear Mary to die.' Of course the second messenger was too late to stop the first. So, on 8 February 1587 Mary, Queen of Scots, prepared to die. She asked for time to put her estate in order but …

> 'The Count of Shrewsbury replied rudely: 'No, no, Madam, you must die, you must die! Be ready between seven and eight in the morning. It cannot be delayed a moment beyond that time.'
>
> *Pierre de Bourdeille, sympathetic French witness*

Beheading was often a very messy business. The decapitation of Mary began with a botch and ended in farce.

1 Mary was not given an appointment with the executioner till the night before.

> 'I am to be executed like a criminal at eight in the morning. I scorn death and vow that I meet it innocent of any crime.'
>
> *Mary, Queen of Scots,*
> *letter to her brother-in-law, King Henry of France*

She stayed awake all night – wouldn't you? She spent the dark hours writing letters and praying. It would have been difficult to sleep anyway with guards marching up and down outside her room and the scaffold being hammered together in the great hall. By the time she got to the block she must have been ready to nod off.

2 Mary's guards refused to let her have a Catholic priest to pray with her. This was a bit spiteful. Instead she was lectured by the Protestant Earl of Kent, who was still trying to convert her when she was on the scaffold.

> 'The Earl of Kent told her that he pitied her greatly to see her thus the victim of the superstition of past ages, advising her to carry the cross of Christ in her heart rather than in her hand.'
>
> *Pierre de Bourdeille*

She simply said …

> 'I've lived a Catholic, so I will die a Catholic.'

This didn't stop Kent going on and on.

3 Mary's servants read a Bible story with her. It was the story of the good thief who died on the cross alongside Jesus. Mary heard it and said, 'That thief was a great sinner – but not such a great sinner as I have been.' Maybe she was thinking of Darnley's bomb.

4 The queen was not allowed to die quietly: 300 people crowded into the hall to witness her execution. The scaffold was decorated in a delightful shade of black and it made a very pleasant day out for the spectators. Some reported that her expression was one of 'smiling cheer', so that was all right.

5 The axeman asked her to forgive him – that was what executioners usually did. Mary did more and thanked him for 'making an end to all my troubles'. She probably hoped this would help his aim. It didn't.

> 'The executioner, or rather the minister of Satan, strove to kill not only her body but also her soul, and kept interrupting her prayers.'
>
> *Pierre de Bourdeille*

6 Mary was dressed in black until the time came for her to die. She took her dress off and was wearing a red petticoat. It symbolized Catholic martyrdom. The crowd gasped. When the executioner attempted to help, she snapped, 'Nay, my good man, touch me not!' She slipped on red sleeves and was all in red, so the blood wouldn't show. She jested that she had never undressed in front of such a crowd. She wore a turban round her head to keep her hair out of the way of the axe. Her eyes were bound with a white cloth, trimmed in gold. Like Lady Jane Grey before her, she now had trouble finding the block. She placed her hands on the block, which put them in danger of being chopped off too …

> 'Then, groping for the block, she laid down her head, putting her chin over the block with both her hands, which, holding there still, had been cut off had they not been espied.'
>
> *Wynkfield*

7 The axeman's assistant held her body steady while the axe fell. It missed the neck and cut into the back of her head. Her servants later said they heard her mutter, 'Sweet Jesus.' The second chop was a better shot but it still needed a bit of sawing with the axe to finish it off.

> 'She endured two strokes of the axe: and so the executioner cut off her head, saving one little gristle.'
>
> *Wynkfield*

8 Traitors always had their heads held up for the spectators to look at. The executioner would cry out, 'May all traitors die this way!' Mary's executioner picked up the head by the hair … but no one told him Mary was wearing a wig. The head slipped out and bounced over the scaffold. The queen's indignity in death was not over …

> 'With her wig off her head, it appeared as grey as one of threescore and ten years old, cropped very short, her face in a moment being so much altered from the form she had when she was alive, as few could remember her by her dead face. Her lips stirred up and down a quarter of an hour after her head was cut off.'
>
> *Wynkfield*

The executioner was a bit upset and he forgot his lines. The Protestant Dean of Peterborough was left to cry out, 'So perish all the queen's enemies.' He forgot to mention Mary's Catholicism, so the Earl of Kent felt the need to come to the dead body and declare, 'Such end all of the queen's and the Gospel's enemies.' They ranted and canted over her corpse to score political points.

9 Mary's pet dog, a Skye terrier, had slipped into the hall under the cover of her skirts and was still hiding there when her head was lopped off. It finally came out, whimpering.

> 'Yet afterward it would not depart from the dead corpse, but came and lay between her head and her shoulders.'
>
> *Wynkfield*

It's said that the dog refused to eat and pined away and died.

10 Mary's heart was removed – the English didn't want any of that Robert the Bruce nonsense with loyal Scots following a heart into battle. The heart was buried in the castle grounds and hasn't been seen since. Mary asked to be buried in France. So, of course, she was buried in Peterborough, which is not quite the same thing at all. In 1612 her son, by then James I of England, had her coffin moved to Westminster Abbey, where it remains today.

Meanwhile, in the grounds of Fotheringhay Castle the Scottish national flower, the thistle, was growing. People said they sprang from the tears of Mary, Queen of Scots.

– AFTERMATH –

Mary had done her best to die with dignity. But squabbles with the executioner about the ownership of her cross spoiled the occasion – it was made from the wood of Christ's cross (she believed) and decorated in gold. The executioner lusted after it.

She wasn't even permitted to have her servants care for her corpse after execution. The Earl of Kent, stony as ever, said …

> ‘Madam, that cannot well be granted, for that it is feared lest some of them would seek to wipe their napkins in some of your blood, which were not convenient.’
>
> *Sheriff of Nottingham, witness report*

Martyr’s blood was highly prized by believers.*

Elizabeth received news of the execution with surprise and horror, it is said. We have to wonder why. On Valentine’s Day she wrote to King James of Scotland, Mary’s son, to express her regrets. The words ‘brass’ and ‘neck’ come to mind. Elizabeth said …

> 14 February 1587
>
> My dear Brother, I would you knew (though not felt) the extreme dolour that overwhelms my mind, for that miserable accident which (far contrary to my meaning) hath befallen. I beseech you that as God and many more know, how innocent I am in this case.
>
> Beseeching God to send you a long reign.
>
> Your most assured loving sister and cousin,
>
> ELIZAB. R

Unbelievable.

Mary’s execution would not go unavenged. Elizabeth could lie to James in Scotland, but could she lie to the God she believed in? For God said,

* Blood-soaked mementoes were also prized by the ghoulish souvenir hunters. When Charles I was beheaded there was a rush to dabble in the red stuff … and he was hardly a martyr.

> 'It is mine to avenge; I will repay. In due time their foot will slip; their day of disaster is near and their doom rushes upon them.'
>
> *Deuteronomy 32:35*

So God sent the Spanish Armada to act as his avengers … then God changed his/her mind and s/he destroyed the Armada? How fickle is that?

— THE IRISH PROBLEM —

Elizabeth's English subjects saw Ireland as a territory and a population to be conquered and civilized, much as the Spanish conquistadors of the same century saw South America. Elizabeth called the Irish 'vile rebels'. Sir John Davies, the Irish Attorney General, said …

> 'A barbarous country must first be broken by war before it will be capable of good government.'

Elizabeth's governor, the Earl of Sussex, said …

> 'I have often wished Ireland could be sunk in the sea.'

Towards the end of Elizabeth's reign, Lord Lieutenant Essex wrote that …

> 'Reformation and total conquest was the only way to subdue Ireland.'

No room for negotiation then, chaps?

Many Irish lived on the threshold of starvation – they had little to lose by risking their lives in rebellion. It was a hatred born of hunger.

In 1569 when a rebellion had broken out among the 'Wild Irish', the English commander murdered innocent farmers who weren't rebelling against anyone. His logic?

> 'If they're dead they can't produce food to feed our enemies.'

In 1573 Elizabeth's Lord Deputy, Sir Henry Sidney, wrote to the queen's council about the deaths of Irish varlets:

> 'I assure you that the number of them is great, and some of the best, and the rest tremble for the most part. Down they go in every corner and down they shall go.'

The following year 50 O'Moores of Laois were treacherously killed, having agreed to attend a 'parley' with crown officials at Mullaghmast. It was a lesson in how to cheat at war.

- The English invited their Irish enemies to dinner.
- The hosts disguised their soldiers as servants.
- When their guests sat down to eat, they had them stabbed to death.

Seventeen Irish leaders died that way.*

The ambush had been carried out in accordance with an order signed by Sidney. The leading murderer was given a knighthood. Of course.†

---

* History is full of examples of dinner invites ending with funeral invites. If the Irish had been as good at history as they were at war, they might have declined the invite.

† Sidney's time as Lord Deputy had been a thankless age for him. Elizabeth

> 'The enemy of my enemy is my friend.'
>
> *Arabian or Chinese saying*

In 1580 Elizabeth was enraged when the Irish invited the Spanish to land in Ireland. Only 600 of Philip I's men landed and were captured immediately. The English executed 500 of them in cold blood. Looks as if the Spanish would get a lot of sympathy from the Irish. Yet, in 1588 when Spanish survivors of the failed Armada raid were shipwrecked in Ireland, many were massacred by their hosts, the 'Wild Irish' peasants.

The 'Old English' Catholics who lived in Ireland detested the Gaelic Irish. The effect of Elizabeth's persecution was remarkable … the enemies united against her.

There were no less than six separate rebellions in a short space of time. The Irish had little to lose. In 1583 Sir Philip Sydney visited Ulster and spent the night in a peasant's home and wrote …

> 'Half a dozen children, almost naked, were sleeping on a little straw with a pig, a dog, a cat, two chickens and a duck. The poor woman spread a mat on a chest, the only piece of furniture in the house and invited me to lie there. The animals greeted the first ray of the sun with their cries and began to look for something to eat … I got up very soon for fear of being devoured.'

---

felt that he was too ambitious and in 1578 unjustly charged him with wasting her money. He had spent too much of his personal fortune in Ireland and his son Philip was penniless. Sidney's health had suffered from the Irish campaigns. On retirement, he described himself as being 'fifty-four years of age, toothless and rambling and £5,000 in debt'.

In 1594 the Nine Years War started (and would end nine years later – such a coincidence). The Irish Chief Hugh O'Neill led the rebels against Elizabethan rule. In 1598 Ulster joined in the war and Hugh O'Neill beat the English at Yellow Ford – that's a place in County Armagh, not the car he was driving at the time.

Did you know … the Pirate Queen

Grace O'Malley (1530–1603) was born into a family of Irish sailors and traders … though some of their activities were seen as piracy by the authorities. Certainly they would demand either cash or a portion of the cargo in exchange for safe passage through their waters on the West Coast of Ireland.

Grace wanted to be a sailor like the rest of her family. But her father told the young girl, 'Your long hair would tangle in the ropes.'

Grace was furious. She dressed like a boy and hacked her hair till it was short as a sailor's. Sorted. She told her father she was ready to sail with him. Her family laughed and gave her a new nickname: Grainne Mhaol (Grace the Bald). Her father gave in and they set sail for Spain. On the way they were attacked by an English ship. Her father told her to get safely below the decks. Instead she climbed up a mast. From her perch she spotted an enemy creeping up behind her father with a knife raised.

Grace dropped onto the man's back, kicking, biting and screaming. The terrified man fled and so did the rest of the English. She had saved her father's life.

She married the vicious Donal O'Flaherty – it was said he murdered his sister's stepson when he thought the boy was getting too much power.

In 1593 her sons were arrested as rebels so Grace went to London to petition Queen Elizabeth for their release.* The two women were nearly the same age – about 60 – when they met at Greenwich Palace.

Grace wore a fine gown, but had a hidden dagger. Guards found it before she could attack the queen. Grace said she only had the dagger to defend herself. Queen Elizabeth believed her.

Grace refused to bow down to Elizabeth because, she said, Elizabeth wasn't the queen of Ireland. Still Elizabeth liked Grace O'Malley and they reached an agreement – Elizabeth would dismiss her unpopular Irish governor, Grace would refrain from rebellion. They each kept their promise for a while but reneged on the agreement shortly after.

Both women died in the year 1603.

As the Nine Years War dragged on the Earl of Essex was sent to quell the rebellion once and for all – his failure led to his downfall and his decapitation. The English were happy to try a nasty old weapon – famine. They burned the Irish crops and stopped next year's being planted. By 1602 Irish bodies lay in ditches, mouths stained green from trying to eat nettles.

* It seems likely they spoke Latin as the common language.

DANGEROUS DAYS DEATH V

MALNUTRITION

Starvation is where the body expends more energy than it takes in. To continue to live, the body has to break down existing muscle and fat for food, especially as glucose is needed for the all-important brain. Basically, you eat yourself to death from the inside out, finally breaking down critical organs until you die. Assuming of course you continue to have no food.

As your fat and muscle are converted into energy you gradually waste away. The feeling of hunger fades as your stomach shrinks. You become weaker and weaker, too weak even to drink, and dehydration sets in. Your skin becomes cracked and any movement is painful – not that you have the energy to move. A bag of skin, bone and wasted diet books, you die.

Without water, death takes only three to ten days, with water four to six weeks, but if you're really fat anything up to six months.

Dr Peter Fox

In 1603 Elizabeth pardoned the defeated Hugh O'Neill … then she died. But she'd succeeded in wiping out most of Ireland's old chiefs. Her legacy – the dispossession of Irish landowners by the 'plantation' of Protestant settlers – would cause pain for hundreds of years.

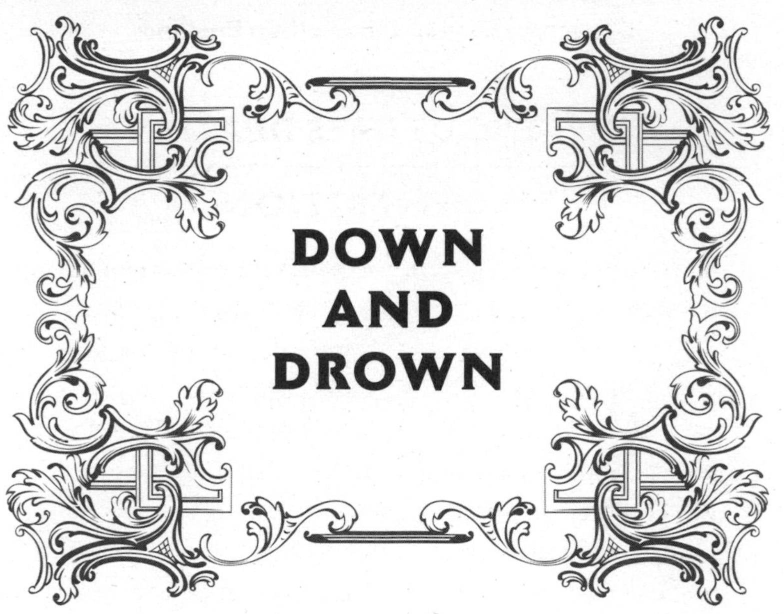

DOWN AND DROWN

— THE FATED FAVOURITES —

> 'And I ordered Mary's execution. I murdered God's anointed queen. And now God's most dutiful son makes Holy War to punish me.'
>
> *Hollywood script* Elizabeth: The Golden Age *(2007)*

Mary, Queen of Scots, had been Catholic so the Catholic Spanish king sent the Armada fleet to invade and avenge her execution.

The Armada is portrayed as a classic case of the plucky little underdog (the English navy) defeating the superior (but nasty) force, the overdog* that was Spain. David versus Goliath. Sunderland versus Leeds (1973 cup final), 100-to-1 Foinavon against all odds (1967 Grand National), tortoise

---

* Technically there is no such word. But logic says that if there's an underdog it has to be under an overdog.

versus hare, Cinderella … the list is endless. In fact there are so many tales of underdog triumphs we tend to forget the superior force almost always wins – *Titanic* versus iceberg was only ever going to have one victor.

So what went wrong with the Spanish plan to crush little England?

Philip's fatalism

> 'The true adventurer goes forth aimless and uncalculating to meet and greet unknown fate.'
>
> *O. Henry (1862–1910), American writer*

Why was Philip's fancy the favourite in this two-horse race? His plan had more flaws than the Empire State Building. The doom clues were there from the start …

The Marquis of Santa Cruz was in charge of preparing the Armada ships. The invading troops were under the command of the Duke of Parma. The latter boasted he could take London within eight days of landing. All he wanted was the element of surprise. King Philip pointed out that building and sailing 700 massive troop carriers would be difficult to keep secret. 'You are having a larf, Parma,' must have been his reaction. Philip's own suggestion was to make diversionary attacks on the coasts of Ireland and Wales.

Philip wasn't sure of the loyalty of Parma, his commander in the war against the rebellious Dutch colony. There were rumours that Elizabeth, who supported the Dutch rebels, was promising Parma the crown of the Netherlands if he became a turncoat.

Philip was also quarrelling with Santa Cruz. He kept urging the admiral to attack but Santa Cruz wanted his older ships properly refitted and new ones built. Then Santa Cruz and Parma were often at odds with one another. The Spanish high command were not playing happy families.

The war aims were confused. What would happen if they battled their way through to London? Could they impose Spanish rule over the whole of England? Could they put Philip's daughter Isabella on the throne? Unlikely. Parma had a secret Plan B: order Elizabeth to grant tolerance to English Catholics and keep her nose out of the Netherlands conflict. Oh, and tell that naughty Mr Drake to stop attacking our treasure ships.

Did you know ... Drake's wisdom

Drake attacked the Spanish fleet in Cadiz harbour on 29 April 1587. He destroyed around 30 ships and their supplies. It meant the Armada could not sail that year – it bought time for England.

Drake famously said he had, 'singed the King of Spain's beard'. But that wasn't a boast as it's usually portrayed. Drake knew beards soon grow again. The Armada was delayed not defeated. He was being a realist not a braggart.

1587 rolled into 1588 and Philip wanted a high-level investigation into the failure of the Armada to set sail. Then Admiral Santa Cruz really let the side down. He fell ill and took the final Cruz cruise ... he died. Philip was philosophical. Brutally unfeeling and in the worst possible taste – but philosophical. He remarked ...

> 'God has shown me favour by removing Santa Cruz now rather than when the Armada was at sea.'*

Any other person would have said, 'God is trying to tell me to quit.' Santa Cruz was replaced by the Duke of Medina Sidonia in February 1588. The duke was not a natural choice. He protested …

> 'I know by the small experiences I have had afloat that I soon become sea-sick.'

Not an auspicious start. The Spanish crews would soon be discouraged if they saw their admiral expressing Technicolor yawns.

The grand plan was to sail from Spain with 9,000 men and join up with Parma's 30,000. But Parma's force had been reduced to 18,000 after an attritional Dutch winter. The invaders were under-strength.

Parma was now getting feet as cold as the North Atlantic. He questioned the feasibility of his Dutch troops sailing out to meet the Spanish Armada force. What if they were intercepted before the mighty Spanish galleons and galleasses smashed the English fleet? Parma ham is renowned. This was Parma chicken …

> 'If we were to come across any of the English ships they could destroy us with the greatest of ease. This must be obvious, and neither the valour of our men nor any other human effort could save us.'

---

* Never mind, he probably sent a kind message to Santa Cruz's family saying, 'Our thoughts are with you at your time of grief … blah … blah…'

It's hard to know what colour the cuckoos were on Philip's planet, but he was not of this earth when he replied …

> 'Victory is a gift of God. He grants it or takes it away as he wills. We can expect him to assist us unless we become unworthy through our sins.'

So Philip was saying, 'Be a good Catholic boy, go to church, say your prayers and we can't lose.' If he really believed that, why bother with tactics at all? As one of Philip's commanders put it cynically …

> 'So we are sailing in the confident hope of a miracle.'

If Philip's forces had no confidence it's easy to see why the Armada wasn't quite the Goliath it is made out to be in school books. The Spanish force WOULD be formidable if it landed. England was placing its faith in defeating the invader on the seas.

Fatalist Phil had failed to prepare properly, but England was in a potentially perilous position. They made the most of their resources …

> 'When fate hands you a lemon, make lemonade.'
>
> *Dale Carnegie (1888–1955), American writer*

The cruel sea

> 'Far better it is to dare mighty things, to win glorious triumphs, even though checkered by failure, than to rank with those poor spirits who neither enjoy much nor suffer much, because they live in the grey twilight that knows not victory nor defeat.'
>
> *Theodore Roosevelt (1858–1919), US President*

And so they set sail. The greatest fleet the world had ever seen, heading for the rocks – metaphorically and physically.

- A lack of wind delayed the voyage from Spain. The men aboard ate the provisions and began to suffer disease. The stores were turning rotten and the water foul. An outbreak of typhus weakened crews on the warships.* The longer they were forced to stay out at sea, the less effective they became. Coughs and chills, pains in the joints, rashes and headaches are enough to impair anyone's fighting spirit.

* A delightful disease spread from person to person by body lice. Just make sure you check your body for lice every night and you should be fine.

- The Spanish waited for fresh supplies to replace the rotten food they'd had to throw overboard.*
- Philip fancied himself as a great strategist. While he wouldn't be tasting the salty tang of sea-spray for himself, he was happy to impose rules on those who would. He told Medina Sidonia, 'DON'T engage the English fleet before you meet up with Parma's force. And DON'T secure an anchorage in England.' Daftly dangerous decisions.
- When the Armada made its stately way along the south coast of England, the English admiral, Lord Charles Howard, allowed it to pass his Western Squadron, waiting in Plymouth. Howard and his vice-admiral, Sir Francis Drake, weren't going to confront the Spanish, they were going to follow and harass them. With the westerly wind behind them, the English were manoeuvrable enough to float like a butterfly and sting like a bee.† They stalked their prey. The English Eastern Squadron lay in wait in the Straits of Dover. Come into my parlour, said the spider to the fly …

---

* As the English fleet lay in wait, strangely, they too were short of provisions, despite being in home ports. Admiral Lord Howard wrote that the ships in Plymouth had just 18 days of provisions and in port the cupboard was bare. An incentive to win quickly then, lads. The other incentive was the propaganda that said Spanish invaders would torture and burn English Protestants.

† To be honest, Muhammad Ali's metaphor is flawed. Drop a butterfly in a bucket of water and it may well 'float' … but it won't go very far. It will float like blotting paper. Maybe we should rewrite the great quote to read, 'Flit like a butterfly, sting like a bee'?

Did you know ... bowling along

Every child used to know the tale of Sir Francis Drake playing bowls as the Armada hove into sight.* 'We have time to finish the game and beat the Spanish too,' he said.

The first recorded report of his daring defiance came 40 years after the event. Those famous words were added over 150 years later, so their provenance is as suspect as that Van Gogh painting at your local car boot sale.

But records DO show the tide was against Drake's fleet setting out. It wouldn't be possible to sail till that evening – and, anyway, the Armada was progressing at 2 mph. Elizabeth on a Zimmer frame could have caught them at will. So it WOULD have been feasible for him to shrug and bowl on.

 The Spanish were at a disadvantage. The English sailors knew the local waters. The English guns fired 4 shots an hour to the Spanish one. The Spanish oar-and-sail-powered galleasses were fearsome fighters but had weak rudders that could disable themselves without English help. And, to cap it all, the summer of 1588 was one of the stormiest in living memory. God was a Protestant that year.

* Every child knew it until a National Curriculum decided it was more important for the youth of England to learn about Nazi Germany. Well, it's popular, so let's Reich while the iron's hot?

Did you know … dad's Tudor army

The Home Guard was not an invention of World War II. Elizabethan England set up 'Trained Bands' under the command of local gentlemen. Some TBs, like the London one, were efficient and effective. Those in the far-flung regions, however, tended to be under-equipped and under-prepared. Even on the south-east 'front line', a third of the men were armed with old bows and arrows.

If Spain's battle-hardened veteran troops had landed, the 'Trained Bands' would most likely have ended up under six feet of English soil … probably shortly after crying, 'Don't panic, Captain Mainwaring, don't panic!'

On 31 July 1588 the Armada inflicted heavy losses … on themselves. Two ships collided and one, *Rosario*, damaged her steering. As it was being fixed, another ship, *San Salvador*, exploded and blew off its stern. Some 200 Spanish perished … along with a lot of the money chests that held the pay for the invaders. Then the *Rosario*, with its shaky steering, managed to collide with yet another ship. The English looked on as the Spanish stumbled round like drunken bull-fighters in a china store. *Rosario* was abandoned and Spanish morale sank.

Did you know … explosion on the *San Salvador*

Conspiracy theories are not new. There was a massive explosion on the *San Salvador*. What happened? An accident with gunpowder, you would think. But other stories added intrigue to the tragedy. They included …

- a German gunner was peeved because a Spanish officer reprimanded him, so he blew up the ship in revenge. OR …
- a German gunner's wife was sneaked on board illicitly. When she was attacked, he blew up the ship in revenge.

Crazy theories? Yes … except one of the survivors is listed as a German woman.

That same evening, Medina Sidonia wrote to Parma in the Netherlands asking for a pilot to guide him through the Dutch shoals to their rendezvous. His postscript summed up the image of English tactics that has become legendary …

> 'The English continue to harass our rear. Their ships have increased to over 100. Some are excellent vessels and all are very fast sailors. Their ships are so fast and nimble, they can do anything they like with them.'
>
> *The Duke of Medina Sidonia, dispatch 31 July 1588*

On the shores of England the defenders waited. On 6 August the Earl of Leicester suggested Her Majesty visit the troops at Tilbury … which she would do on 18 August when the danger of invasion had passed. Other councillors were urging her to pack up and leave London so that a Spanish landing would not find her. She declined.

On 7 August the Spanish headed for Calais in search of Parma and his Flanders' troops. Both sides were running low on ammunition as the skirmishes continued up the English Channel. Sidonia reached Calais and the Armada dropped anchor. He was told Parma would be ready with the invasion force … in about a fortnight. The English didn't want to wait. They were busily preparing to send in fire-ships to scatter the Spanish fleet. The idea of these 'hell-burners' brought terror to the hearts of the Spanish – they'd seen their destructive power earlier in the year at Antwerp. Panic? They were frantic with fear.

> 'Eight English ships, with all sail set and a fair wind and tide, came straight towards our fleet, all burning fiercely.'
>
> *Spanish eyewitness*

In the small hours of 8 August the English brought the Spanish nightmare into the waking world. Fire-ships plunged towards the anchored Armada. Loaded cannon began to explode as they reached the Spanish galleons. Spanish captains cut the cables on their best anchors and fled. Most evaded the fire-ships but were carried into the North Sea with poor substitute anchors failing to stop them. Sidonia wanted them to re-form, but the tide-swept galleons were scattered. And, it's said, a lot of Spanish captains had argued against stopping in Calais – they simply disregarded orders, probably muttering into their beards, 'I told you so.'

- At daybreak on 8 August the English struck at Gravelines, near Dunkirk. Some Spanish ships had no ammunition left, some sank and others were driven ashore by hostile winds. A thousand Spanish and a handful of English sailors died so that Elizabeth could live.

- By 9 August the wind had swung to the south to blow the limping Armada northwards up the east coast of England. Discipline among the defeated was breaking down. Meanwhile, on shore, Parma had begun to march his invasion forces up to the barges. But when he heard the news of the Gravelines disaster, like the Grand Old Duke of York, he marched them down again. His dismal escort Armada was in pieces – in every sense.

> 'We feared ourselves lost or captured by the enemy or the whole Armada drowned on the sandbanks. It was the most fearful day in the world. The whole company had lost hope and foresaw only death.'
>
> *Luis de Miranda – Sidonia staff officer*

 As the Spanish sailed the long way home – around the north coast of Scotland then down the west coast of Ireland – the English followed like police escorting drunken troublemakers off the premises. The English had little powder and shot to inflict more damage, but God had the winds that would wreak havoc on the tattered Armada. Struck by the tail of an Atlantic hurricane, 28 Spanish ships foundered off the West Coast of Ireland … the weather inflicting far more damage than the English navy had managed.* The English struck a medal to celebrate their God's victory over the Catholics. The inscription summed up the smirking triumphalism of the victors …

> 'Jehovah blew with His winds, and they were scattered.'

Philip could only reply (allegedly) …

> 'I sent my ships to fight against the English, not against the elements.'

He could have added that in a fight between his sailors and a cannonball there was only going to be one winner.

---

* Some crew made it ashore to seek refuge with their allies, the native Irish. Many were given succour – others treated like suckers: robbed or massacred. With friends like these …?

What happens when man meets a powder-propelled piece of metal?

DANGEROUS DAYS DEATH VI

CANNON SHOT

Cannon balls carry a lot of energy, so when hit by one a 'soft' person tends to come off worst. You could be 'lucky' and just have a glancing, survivable hit to an arm or leg, but that would tear said limb off instantaneously and very painfully from your body.

More than likely you would get a direct hit to your body which you wouldn't see coming (especially if hit from behind). As it hits, the energy wave from the cannon ball turns the skin and muscle ahead of it to mush, before going on to rip through the underlying bone and organs. Violently torn apart by the force, pieces of you would fly in all directions – and, in a slowly falling mist of red blood, rain on the people around you. With your body reduced to more pieces than a Christmas jigsaw, the only tools required by a doctor would be a shovel, a mop and black bag.

Dr Peter Fox

– THE GLOATING QUEEN –

> 'We are all worms, but I do believe I am a glow-worm.'
>
> *Winston Churchill (1874–1965), British politician and historian*

All was not rosy in the English naval garden … if navies have gardens.* Drake had disobeyed orders when he looted the stricken *Rosario* and was deeply unpopular in some quarters.

But Elizabeth was happy. Her life had been saved.

She visited her unused troops at Tilbury to congratulate them on the brave way they didn't fight and tell them how great she was. She'd defeated the Armada single-handedly, it would seem …

> 'I am come amongst you, as you see, at this time, not for my recreation and disport, but being resolved, in the midst and heat of the battle, to live and die amongst you all; to lay down for my God, and for my kingdom, and my people, my honour and my blood, even in the dust.'
>
> *Elizabeth I speech at Tilbury*

So Elizabeth was sharing her people's dangerous days? She was going into the heat of battle … a week after it was clear that battle was over?

Then she added, famously …

> 'I know I have the body of a weak, feeble woman; but I have the heart and stomach of a king, and of a king of England too, and … I myself will take up arms, I myself will be your general, judge, and rewarder of every one of your virtues in the field.'

---

* Maybe they grow sea anemones?

She will, like an English Joan of Arc, 'take up arms'? Did any of the troops at Tilbury dare to mutter, 'You're a week too late, mate.' Certainly one soldier was later heard to say ...

> 'When the Armada arrived Elizabeth was pissing herself with fear.'

He was punished severely.

The text of this speech was found in a letter dated around 1624 – more than 30 years after it was allegedly spoken. Historians debate whether or not it's genuine. No one seems to mention that (genuine or not) it is tripe of the highest order. It's the most famous quote from an English monarch since Richard III didn't say, 'My kingdom for a horse.' Yet it is hot air.

Elizabeth had no plan to 'die amongst you all' and she certainly wasn't intending to take up arms while there was cannon-fodder like the troops at Tilbury to die in her place. It's codswallop, drivel, bunkum and baloney.*

— THE SPANISH THREAT —

> 'Some made but little account of the Spanish force by sea; but I do warrant you, all the world never saw such a force as theirs was.'
>
> *Lord Howard of Effingham (1510–73), English diplomat*

How great was the threat from the Armada and the troop landings from Flanders?

---

* Maybe that famous quote should read, 'I have the heart and stomach of a king ... but the bladder of an incontinent puppy.'

The defeat of the Armada in 1588 is remembered as a great victory for the English navy. It was also a victory for the English spies, who knew most of Philip's plans before his ships even left Spain. They didn't know when the Armada would sail or where it would land, but they knew the strength of its forces. Beacon bonfires were prepared on hilltops to signal when the invasion started.

The English were ready for the Spanish – whenever they came.

But the Spanish helped in their own downfall. Not only in the poorly led and poorly equipped ships but in the indifferent, disjointed leadership. Their commander, the Duke of Medina Sidonia, summed it up in a letter to Philip …

> 'When Your Majesty ordered me to take command of the Armada, I gave Your Majesty many reasons why I should not do so. This was not because I wanted to refuse. It was because I realized we were attacking a country so powerful, and with so many friends, that we'd need an even bigger force than the one you had gathered together. My health is bad and I am always sea sick. The person in charge of the Armada should understand sailing and fighting at sea. I know nothing of either. Still, you ordered me to sail and I did. We are now half way to England at the port of Corunna and the Armada is already damaged. Many of our largest ships have gone missing. On the ships that remain there are many sick men. The number of sick will grow because of the bad food. Not only is it rotten, but there is so little that it will not last two months. I would ask Your Majesty to decide if we should continue this voyage. Remember the huge army you gathered to attack Portugal – and many of

> the Portuguese were on our side. Well, sire, how can you expect us to attack England with the force that we have now? All of these problems and dangers can be avoided. Simply make peace with the English now.'

The commander of the invading army was the Duke of Parma. He agreed with Admiral Medina Sidonia and also sent a letter to Philip …

> 'The foot soldiers are ready and together. But the horse-soldiers are scattered around the country since there was not enough horse food here. I am doing my best to keep up the spirits of the troops. Still, the foot soldiers only number 18,000. Even with the 6,000 coming with the Armada we will still have a weak force. Sickness will mean we shall have even less. I wish Your Majesty could have let me have more men. We are also short of pilots who know the crossing to England. Without them we could not attempt to invade England.'

Philip said 'No' to these requests … and doomed many unfortunate Spanish soldiers and sailors to suffering and death. Less than half of the 130 ships returned to Spain.

> QUEEN ELIZABETH I: 'Go back to your rat-hole! Tell Philip I fear neither him, nor his priests, nor his armies. Tell him if he wants to shake his little fist at us, we're ready to give him such a bite he'll wish he'd kept his hands in his pockets!'
>
> SPANISH MINISTER: 'You see a leaf fall, and you think you know which way the wind blows. Well, there is a wind coming, madame, that will sweep

away your pride.' [Turns to leave with his ministers]

QUEEN ELIZABETH I: 'I, too, can command the wind, sir! I have a hurricane in me that will strip Spain bare when you dare to try me!'*

Hollywood script of Elizabeth: The Golden Age *(2007)*

— PHILIP'S FATALISM —

'Lay not the blame on me, O sailor, but on the winds. By nature I am as calm and safe as the land itself, but the winds fall upon me with their gusts and gales, and lash me into a fury that is not natural to me.'

Aesop (620–564 BC), Greek fabulist

There is a curious and forgotten story that Philip of Spain believed the Armada *deserved* to fail because God was punishing him. But God's wrath was not, as you might expect, for Philip's involvement in the death of his son.†

No, Philip confessed that when he was married to Mary he had lusted after Elizabeth, 'a fair and beautiful woman'.

Elizabeth had probably been complicit in the flirting with Uncle Tom Seymour and it is pretty certain the minx had given Philip every encouragement.

---

* Amazing. And it was a hurricane that destroyed the Spanish Armada. How prophetic is that? Yes, all right, it was written 420 years *after* the actual event, and Elizabeth never said those words. But if she HAD it would be amazing. No?

† The death of *Philip's* son, not the Son of God. That's another story altogether. You can read it in a history book called 'The Bible', which is a bit like this history book without the jokes.

> 'At the time of Queen Mary's pregnancy Lady Elizabeth contrived to so ingratiate herself with the Spaniards at court, and especially the king, that ever since no one has favoured her more than he does.'
>
> *Giovanni Michiel, Venetian ambassador*

Of course, Philip would go on to attempt the Armada invasion. But was he motivated by a noble desire to avenge the execution of his fellow Catholic Mary, Queen of Scots? Or a more base desire to exorcize his thwarted feelings of love for Elizabeth?

> 'The loss of the Armada was an event to be wept over for ever. It lost us respect and reputation among warlike people, which we used to have. Almost all of Spain went into mourning. People talked about nothing else.'
>
> *Father Jeronimo, Spanish Chronicler (1605)*

— THE FORGOTTEN ARMADAS —

> 'Success does not consist in never making mistakes but in never making the same one a second time.'
>
> *George Bernard Shaw*

Every schoolchild has heard about the Armada, but no one remembers the *second*, *third* and *fourth* Armadas.

Philip, having recovered from the shock of defeat, soon started planning another seaborne invasion. Spain would learn from its mistakes (he decided). The new ships were built along English lines and 126 set off in October 1596.* English attacks delayed the sailing but couldn't stop it. It seemed Phil's luck was in. Elizabeth's ships were mostly in port, being refitted. If Philip had been a footballer this would be an open goal.

But God sent one of his gales (again), sinking 30 Spanish ships and driving the rest back to port.

Would Philip get God's message? No. He decided to try for third time lucky.

In 1597 a third Armada of 136 ships sailed off to crush the English with a new plan. It was mid-October ... again. They would take Falmouth while the bulk of the English fleet was away in the Azores – another open goal. Falmouth would provide the Spanish with a base from which to sail out, refreshed, and smash the returning fleet.

They were 30 miles from Falmouth when a gale wrecked 28 ships and drove the rest back home. It was déjà-vu all over again.

Philip did the sensible thing and died – his conversation with God when he got to Heaven must have been interesting.

And in 1601 a fourth Armada, organized by Philip's son, succeeded ... in landing in Ireland to support the Earl of Tyrone's rebellion. But the rebellion failed and the Spanish surrendered. God had saved his breath that time. He probably didn't have a lot left by then.

---

* You may know nothing about sailing but if you have half a wit you would reckon mid-October is close enough to winter to worry about the weather. Oh, phoolish Phil.

BRIEF TIMELINE – THE GLORY YEARS

1580 Francis Drake back from his round-the-world trip laden with treasure for Elizabeth.

1581 It is now 'treason' to convert to Catholicism – and treason comes with harsh penalties. Yet the Catholic Count of Anjou arrives to finalize a deal to marry Elizabeth. Drake is knighted. Cash for honours is nothing new. The Spanish are furious (again) at England honouring a pirate.

1582 Marriage proposal is off. Count of Anjou goes home.

1583 A Catholic plot by Francis Throckmorton is thwarted. He confesses ... with a little help from the Tower torturers.

1585 A colony of English families are settled in Roanoke in America. They will plant that medicinal herb, tobacco.

1586 Philip II of Spain is planning to invade England with a mighty fleet of ships. Another plot is uncovered to kill Elizabeth and this time there is evidence that Mary, Queen of Scots, is in it up to her neck ...

1587 ... and it is her neck that gets it when she is butchered with two chops and a bit of sawing on the block. Elizabeth is hysterical with grief.*

* A bit late, Liz. You should have thought of the grief when you signed the execution warrant. Maybe the tears are for show?

1588 Philip II launches his Armada against England. He can't beat the weather. Meanwhile favourite Leicester dies leaving Elizabeth grief-stricken (again).

1589 Drake sets off to demolish the remains of the Spanish fleet but half of his 15,000 men die in the attempt. Elizabeth has invested £20k in the venture and is furious.

1590 Roanoke is visited by an English ship. They find the settlement deserted. There is no trace of the 90 men, 17 women, and 11 children, no sign of any struggle or battle. The 'Lost Colony' is a mystery.

— DRAKE'S DODGY DEALINGS —

'Kingston, or Ballantyne the brave,
Or Cooper of the wood and wave—
So be it, also! And may I
And all my pirates share the grave,
Where these and their creations lie.'

*Robert Louis Stevenson (1850–94), Scottish novelist**

Sir Francis Drake is one of those heroes of history whose life doesn't stand up to examination with a magnifying glass … unless that magnifying glass is heavily rose-tinted.

* And author of *Treasure Island* who, along with the three writers he names, is largely responsible for the myth that pirates were romantic rascals rather than barbarous boated bullies with bad breath.

- Drake was an outlaw to the Spanish. Philip is said to have offered a reward, worth about £4 million today, for Drake … dead or alive.

- Drake is remembered for leading the defeat of the Armada. In fact he only led the Western Squadron and almost led it to defeat through his recklessness. How? It had been agreed that Drake would lead the other ships as they followed the Armada along the south coast of England. The English fleet would follow the stern lantern of his *Revenge*. Drake extinguished his lantern and the English fleet scattered as a result. Admiral Howard's war almost ended disastrously when daybreak revealed the lantern he was following was a Spanish ship. Where had Drake gone? He'd gone to board a damaged Spanish galleon and relieve it of its loot. Drake's hero status probably spared him a court martial for disobedience. Howard did not forgive or forget.* Captain Martin Frobisher was Drake's biggest critic …

> 'Sir Francis Drake, like a coward, kept by *Rosario* all night because he would have the plunder. He thinks to cheat us of our share of 15,000 ducats. But we will have our shares or I will make him spend the best blood in his belly.'
>
> *Martin Frobisher (1539–94), English captain*

* Drake and the Spanish captain agreed on the value of the prize money on the Spanish ship. That should go to the queen. Spanish records revealed there was a far greater fortune on board than Drake delivered. So did Drake and the Spanish captain lie about the value and split the profit?

- The Armada staggered back to Spain. Drake was sent to attack the remnants of Phil's fleet in their harbours and finish them off. After some initial success he was diverted by the idea of attacking Lisbon, but only succeeded in causing a Portuguese uprising. He then set off to intercept the annual Spanish treasure convoy, but got a metaphorical bloody nose. He was in disgrace with Elizabeth and her court for quite a few years.

- Ten years before the Armada arrived, Drake had been sent with six ships to rob the Spanish treasure fleet on the west coast of South America. He took along the nobleman Thomas Doughty, who became increasingly irritated at being commanded by a commoner. He whinged about Drake 'the Captain General'. When Doughty's ship became lost Drake took the notion that Doughty was practising witchcraft. When they were finally reunited, Drake tied the nobleman to the mast and struck him, then imprisoned him as 'a witch and a poisoner'. On landing in Argentina, Drake put Doughty on trial for mutiny and treason. Doughty challenged Drake's legal right; Drake claimed to have a letter of authority from Elizabeth … but refused to show it in the court. 'Sorry, I left it on the ship,' he claimed. Hmmmm. Drake and Doughty dined cheerfully together and the next morning the nobleman was beheaded.

- Attacking the Spanish in the Pacific meant sailing around Cape Horn. Only Drake's own ship, the *Golden Hind*, made it through the Straits of Magellan. Elizabeth's investment in Drake's expedition was rewarded when he captured Spanish treasures worth £7 million at today's values. He kept going west till he'd circumnavigated the globe. In 1580 the *Golden Hind* sailed into Plymouth with Drake and 59 surviving crew aboard. They had a valuable cargo of spices as well as that Spanish treasure. Elizabeth's half-share of the cargo exceeded the rest of her income for that entire year. Francis Drake was her blue-eyed boy. The following year she knighted him.*

* Getting a knighthood for making a powerful person rich? James I was quite open about it; he created the title of baronet and sold it to anyone who paid him £1,500. Prime Minister David Lloyd George made cash for honours a way of life in the early twentieth century. In the twenty-first century scandals over cash for honours were still erupting: £10k a knight. Expensive sort of hotel.

STORM AND STARVE

— NAVAL NEGLECT —

> 'If men should not be cared for better than to let them starve and die miserably, we should very hardly get men to serve. I had rather have never penny in the world than they should lack.'
>
> *Lord High Admiral Howard (1536–1624)*

Understandably most of Elizabeth's sailors were dismissed once the danger was over – a standing army and navy is expensive. Less understandably, the men were left to starve in the streets and die of malnutrition while their grateful queen and country looked on.

> 'Ingratitude is the essence of vileness.'
>
> *Immanuel Kant*

It seems incomprehensible that the heroes who defeated the Armada were so quickly forgotten. Who would volunteer if a new invasion threatened? But harsh treatment was the norm for sailors in the dangerous days of Elizabeth I.

Disease spread through the remaining ships. Howard wrote to the queen to complain that almost half of the crew of the *Elizabeth Jonas* had died. He replaced the dead crew with strong young men yet the infection went on 'in greater extremity than ever it did before and they die and sicken faster than ever they did'.

He explained they had been at sea for eight months with no change of clothes and 'no money wherewith to buy it'. In other words the stingy government had let the men die for lack of money – money the men had earned.

It's easy to defend Elizabeth by saying she wasn't aware of the scale of the suffering – that she would have been too remote. The truth is her chief minister, Lord Burghley, had written to the admiral rubbing his hands with glee at the cash saving of the dead sailors' pay …

> 'By death, or by discharging the sick men, there may be spared something in the general pay.'

Elizabeth must have known what was going on in her own treasury.

Yet Gloriana's lustre wasn't tarnished too much in the eyes of the seamen. The sailors believed bad beer was to blame for their illness.

A year later, things were little better. When *Dreadnought* arrived back in Plymouth from a Portuguese expedition there were just 18 men fit enough to man her – the ship had set off with a crew of 300.

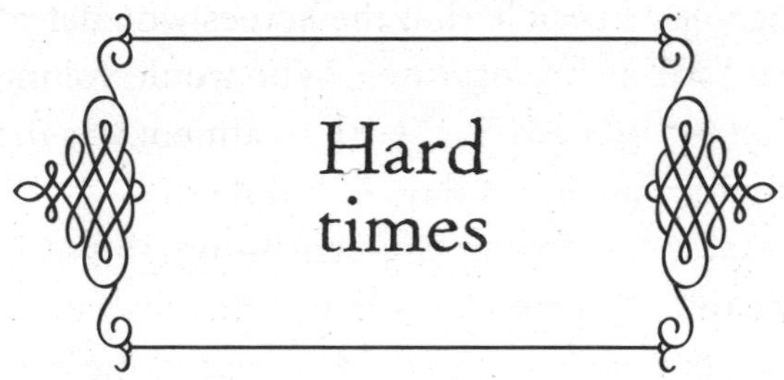

Hard times

> 'Just for the sake of amusement, ask each passenger on the ship to tell you his story, and if you find a single one who hasn't often cursed his life, who hasn't told himself he's the most miserable man in the world, you can throw me overboard head first.'
>
> Candide, *Voltaire*

When Will Shakespeare described England as 'This precious stone set in the silver sea / Which serves it in the office of a wall', he was using a very loose metaphor. That 'wall' may have kept out most invaders, but it wasn't a wall against the diseases that spread around the world.

The Black Death came through the 'wall' in 1348 and ships would carry cholera to Britain 500 years later. The first people to catch the diseases and stagger ashore to infect others would be the sickly sailors, the tainted tars, the bubonic boatmen. It was no fun being a sailor. Look at their sufferings …

1 The crowded crews

'A life on the ocean wave, a home on the rolling deep,
Where the scattered waters rave, and the winds their revels keep!'

*Poem-turned-song by Epes Sargent published 1838**

In the Middle Ages there had been merchant ships. In times of war the navy would commandeer them and mount guns on the decks. But Henry VIII wanted a more efficient navy with purpose-built warships. Cannon were placed between the decks and extra crew were needed to man the guns. Naturally Henry gave little thought to the effect this would have on the swabbies.

On the warships they were now so crushed in badly ventilated spaces even the rats were ratty. In 1545 there was an outbreak of plague and dysentery in the English fleet. If one doesn't get you the other one will.† The surprise is there weren't many more such fleet fatalities.

Did you know ... lying down on the job

There were no toilets as such on Tudor ships. The sailors went to the front of the ship – the 'heads' – where there were grids instead of toilet bowls. The sea washed away most of the filth. But those grids still needed a scrub. That delightful job went each week

---

* Epes didn't write this at sea, you understand. He stood on a New York harbour watching the ships come in. The reality was different. This became a favourite song of that other renowned sailor, Abraham Lincoln.

† 'Plague' sounds worse than dysentery, yet the latter was enough to see a tough warrior like the Black Prince shuffle off his mortal coil in 1376.

to the 'liar'. He was the sailor who was the first to be caught out in a lie on a Monday morning.

Some officers were privileged enough to have their own chamber pot. It would be a hundred years before toilets with seats became a common comfort for sailors.

---

2 The scourge of scurvy

In 1593 Richard Hawkins' crew were struck by scurvy.

> 'It is the plague of the sea and the spoil of mariners.'
>
> *Sir Richard Hawkins (1562–1622), Elizabethan seaman*

A doctor can explain thc progress of the disease …

DANGEROUS DAYS DEATH VII

SCURVY

Scurvy is caused by not having enough vitamin C (ascorbic acid) in your diet, so unless you eat fresh fruit and vegetables containing it you die. Most other animals make their own vitamin C, but humans don't. (We have this in common with guinea pigs, which is why guinea pigs always have a glass of fruit juice at breakfast.)

Vitamin C is used by the body for many things, including the making of collagen, a material which binds, repairs and holds things together – nature's glue! As levels of vitamin C fall you start to feel achy and tired, and your skin becomes rough with spots on the thighs and legs. The repair system starts to fail, wounds heal slowly, you bruise easily and your gums bleed. In the later stages teeth begin to drop out, but by this time you are feeling very unwell with liver and kidney failure, fever and fits. This all takes about three months to happen. So a nice slow, painful crumbling into death – and all for the want of some fruit juice.

Dr Peter Fox

From able seaman to disabled seaman in three months.

> 'The crew lost their strength and could not stand on their feet. Then did their legs swell, their sinews shrink as black as any coal.'
>
> *Jacques Cartier, French explorer, 1535*

We now know scurvy can be cured with vitamin C. To the spongy-gummed sailors, however, scurvy was seen as a curse from God. One group of English sailors was saved when the natives of North America, where they landed, advised them to boil the needles of an eastern white cedar tree.

Sir Richard Hawkins began advocating the use of orange and lemon juice, which helped the sailors enormously.*

* You could call it a lemon-aid. I wouldn't dream of it.

3 Suicide missions

The defeat of the 1588 Armada was not the end of fighting and dying against the Spanish enemies.

Sir Walter Ralegh's cousin, Sir Richard Grenville, had been sent west to capture Spanish treasure ships. Grenville's fleet, led by his ship, the *Revenge*, was ambushed by the Spanish fleet and destroyed on 31 August 1591.

The 50-strong Spanish squadron scattered the 16 English. *Revenge* was surrounded. Grenville's battle against the odds was hampered by having 90 sick sailors in his crew, totally unfit to fight. Sir Richard was hit by a musket ball in the chest. He was having that treated by the ship's surgeon when another hit him in the head. He was captured, but even the Spanish doctors couldn't save him. (The *Revenge* surgeon died too. 'Physician heal thyself,' the Bible advises … but there weren't bullets to the brain in Biblical times.)

Rather than surrender to the Spaniards, Grenville fought to the death against hopeless odds. Victorian poet Alfred Tennyson immortalized the tale in verse …

> 'Sink me the ship, Master Gunner – sink her, split her
> in twain!
> Fall into the hands of God, not into the hands of Spain!'

The bullet had scrambled his brain. Why else would he imagine his surviving crew would commit suicide?

The sailors (who did not have a bullet on the brain) came up with the sensible answer: 'No'.

'And the gunner said "Ay ay", but the seamen made reply:
"We have children, we have wives,
And the Lord hath spared our lives.
We will make the Spaniard promise, if we yield,
to let us go" . . . '

They surrendered and even the hardened Spanish crew found conditions on the little English ship appalling. Grenville died of his wounds, crying, 'Fight on, fight on. No surrender.'

He sounds like Davey Crockett at the Alamo.* In fact, Grenville was brutal, arrogant, ruthless and ambitious. Not really the stuff we expect of movie heroes. Take note, Mr Tennyson.

A prize crew of Spanish sailors headed back to Spain with *Revenge* and its survivors. Ironically, *Revenge* sank in a storm and they were all lost.†

Revenge proselyte Tennyson also coined the phrase 'Nature, red in tooth and claw'. Nature's teeth and claws had achieved what a fleet of Spanish galleons failed to do and sank the ship.

---

* A Mexican claimed that Crockett's body was found in the defeated US fortress surrounded by 'no less than sixteen Mexican corpses', with Crockett's knife buried in one of them. He is remembered in 22 movies where he's been played by actors from Johnny Cash to (inevitably) John Wayne. What a hero.

† As Tennyson put it so poetically, 'And the whole sea plunged and fell on the shot-shattered navy of Spain.' Try reciting 'shot-shattered navy of Spain' aloud with a mouthful of crisps.

4 Stormy weather

Elizabethan sailors were at the mercy of the weather. Storms can sweep you overboard or sink your ship and leave you to drown. There were no lifejackets and no sonar equipment to warn of rocks and shoals. There were maps, of course, but if you weren't entirely sure of your position you could hit a rock and find out your exact position the hard way.

There were ways to reduce the risk of storms … perhaps.

Whistling would bring bad luck. A whistle is a challenge to the wind itself – the wind has the intellectual property on whistling and you'll annoy it if you infringe its copyright. In retribution, the wind will whip up a storm.

Women are equally bad luck on board a ship *unless* they are naked. A naked woman calms the sea. A carved, bare-breasted woman on the prow of the ship will shame the sea into behaving itself.

Watch your language. Some words must be avoided. Words like 'drowned' and 'goodbye'. If someone says 'good luck' to you, it will only bring you bad luck. (Rather as actors believe saying 'Break a leg' will avoid such an eventuality.) The surest way to reverse the curse is by drawing blood. A punch in the nose of the well-wisher ought to do it … and teach them a lesson at the same time.

Be careful who you meet on the way to your ship. If you see a red-haired person it's bad luck. Other bad embarkment omens include a black bag, a priest and a cross-eyed or flat-footed person.

Never kill an albatross or you'll end up like Samuel Taylor Coleridge's 'Ancient Mariner'. And we all know what happened to him. No? As penance for albatrossicide, the old sailor is forced to wander the earth, telling his story repeatedly. (He was also cursed by being the subject of the worst schoolteacher joke ever. Teachers since the mists of time have jested, 'The Ancient Mariner was a terrible goalkeeper … we know this because the poem begins: 'It is an ancient Mariner, And he stoppeth one of three.' Ho! Ho! Laugh? I thought I'd never start.)

Remember, remember …

The misery of ship-borne disease in England has to be put into perspective. Look at the sufferings of the rest of the world.

In the 1490s the Spanish treasure-seekers and conquistadors took native slaves and Indies gold but left behind European diseases. The natives of Haiti numbered around a million. Then Columbus and his successors landed. By the time Elizabeth came to the throne in the 1550s there was not one left – one million to zero in 60 years – devastated by smallpox and influenza.

The rest were brutally (and needlessly) massacred by the Spaniards. Human greed, the greatest plague of all. Maybe those Spanish depredations should moderate our pity for the Spanish victims of English privateers like Drake. The Spanish bought the treasure with native blood and then paid for it with their own blood.

---

5 Painful punishments

> 'Lawless are they that make their wills their law.'
>
> *William Shakespeare*

If the diseases didn't get you then the officers might. Discipline was firm.

- Swearing or blasphemy might earn you a one penny fine.
- Sleeping on duty or stealing could get you a ducking in the cold Atlantic.

> 'Good heavens, a piece of knotted string asleep at his post. Get up you rotten twine!'
>
> *Neddy Seagoon, character in* The Goon Show, *script by Spike Milligan and Larry Stephens (1956)*

- Disobey a direct order? Then you can be tied to the mast and flogged.
- Whatever you do, you mustn't strike an officer. The hand that struck the blow may be sliced off … if you are lucky. A less merciful captain would simply hang you.

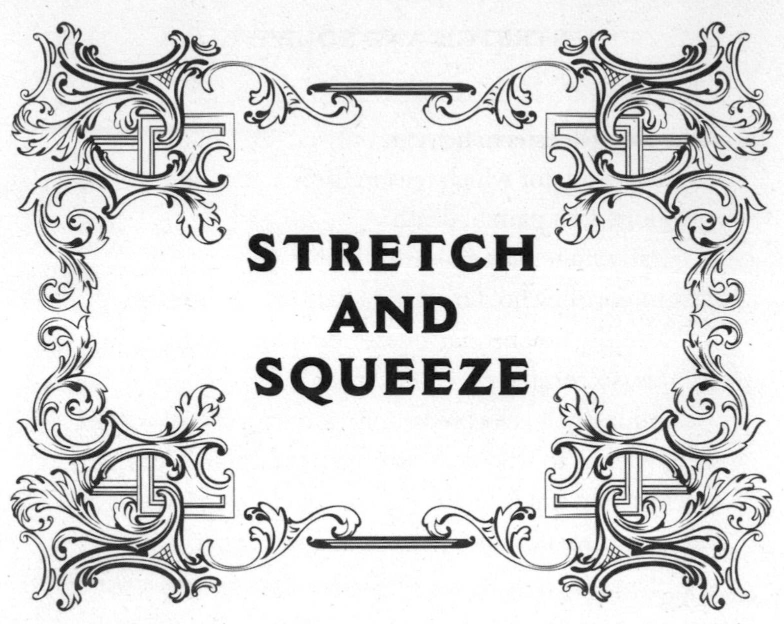

STRETCH AND SQUEEZE

— PARANOIA PALACE —

By the end of the century Elizabeth was over 65. No great age by today's standards, but Elizabeth's body was failing and she knew it. Her taste for marzipan had rotted her teeth, the lead make-up was weakening her ever-sickly constitution. The main thing keeping her alive was a fierce determination not to die.

Don't even THINK about her death, let alone discuss it. Just as Henry VIII had made it treasonable to speculate on his death so Elizabeth believed, 'If you don't talk about it then it won't happen' …

> 'The English esteem her, not only as their queen but as their God, for which reason three things are prohibited on pain of death.
>
> Firstly none may enquire whether she is still a virgin, for they hold her too holy to admit of doubt.
>
> Secondly no one may question her government or estates, so completely is she trusted.
>
> And lastly it is forbidden on pain of death to make enquiries as to who is to succeed her on her decease, for fear that if it were known, this person in his lust for government might plot against the queen's life.'
>
> Travels in England, *Thomas Platter*

Who do you think you are kidding, Mr Platter? Everyone knows James VI of Scotland (son of Mary, Queen of Scots) is going to inherit. And everyone knows he won't invade – a couple of his ancestors tried that and died.

Why invade? His spies will tell him how Elizabeth is failing. He just has to bide his time. Much cheaper.*

And is she really loved by the Catholics or the Puritans? Or do they just hide their contempt for her under the cloak of a discreet silence? Are they not, like James, biding their time?

If they loved her that much how come there were so many plots?

---

* Not that this is casting racist aspersions on a mean Scottish king. Not in this book. I still recoil at the memory of the angry McReader's letter saying, 'Sir, if you print any more jokes about Scotsmen I shall cease borrowing your books.'

BRIEF TIMELINE – THE GREAT DECLINE

1591 Robert Cecil, son of Lord Burghley, is knighted and will rise through the ranks to be top advisor to Elizabeth. James VI of Scotland – obvious heir to the English throne – is enjoying torturing and executing alleged witches. The extreme Puritans are giving the queen as big a headache as the Catholics.

1592 Walter Ralegh (who did not invent the bicycle) is arrested for seducing a lady-in-waiting to the queen.* Meanwhile Elizabeth's pirates have looted £800k of Spanish treasure from the Spanish but pocketed it for themselves. Ralegh is released to recover the stolen-stolen cash.

1593 From December 1592 until December 1593 Stow (the Elizabethan archivist) reports 10,675 plague deaths in London, a city of approximately 200,000 people. Theatres are closed to prevent the spread. They'll open again, so all's well that ends well. Thomas Kyd, playwright, is arrested on charges of writing a slanderous play. He is tortured and branded with hot irons before he is released. Kit Marlowe, part-time spy and playwright, is killed with a knife to the eye in a tavern squabble. Dangerous profession you've chosen, Will Shakespeare.

---

* Maid-in-waiting, Bess Throckmorton, was a ward of the queen, so marrying Ralegh without permission was a crime. They were BOTH locked up. They were devoted. When Ralegh was beheaded in 1616 it's said Bess had his head embalmed and carried it around with her for the rest of her life. Sweet.

1594 With Marlowe dead, Shakespeare is the most experienced playwright in town and in demand. It's an ill wind, etc. And it's plot-against-the-queen time again. Her physician, the Jewish Dr Lopez, is accused of a poison plot by her favourite, the Earl of Essex, and executed … on no real evidence.

Young poet Will Shakespeare has success with violent poems like *The Rape of Lucrece* and even more violent plays like *Titus Andronicus*. The Elizabethans like their entertainments steeped in gore.

1596 Sir Francis Drake, scourge of the Spanish fleets, dies of dysentery after a failed treasure raid in Panama. He is buried at sea. Back home, his drum is said to beat when England is in danger and he will rise to save his country again.

1597 Lord Essex plays the pirate game and sets off to intercept Spanish treasure ships. He returns after failing miserably.

1598 Elizabeth's chief advisor and support for 40 years has been Lord Burghley. He dies, in spite of the queen's nursing efforts – she was feeding him with a spoon at the end.

Parliament creates transportation to the colonies as a new punishment.

1599 Now Essex charges off to Ireland with 16,000 men to put down a rebellion. He is in trouble when he not only fails but negotiates a peace settlement. He's imprisoned for a month and disgraced.

The Globe Theatre opens on the bank of the Thames.

— DEATH OF A DOCTOR —

'Whenever a doctor cannot do good, he must be kept from doing harm.'

Hippocrates (c. 460–377 BC), ancient Greek physician

Elizabeth wielded so much power it attracted the ambitious, like wasps around a jam-jar seeking a share of the sweetness for themselves. What could you do to inveigle your way into her favour? Play on her weaknesses, of course.

She was ageing but still vain enough to think herself attractive. Towards the end of her life the queen refused to have a mirror in any of her rooms. She just wanted to hear how beautiful she was. The door was open to flatterers like the Earl of Essex.

She was also living in fear of her life. So a flatterer who could save her from some plot would get first lick of that jam. Again, young Essex was the man for the job.

'If you live with death threats, you need friends. So you have to risk that they might spy on you.'

Herta Müller (1953—), German-Romanian novelist

Essex's problem was that there wasn't a convenient plot against the queen. So he decided to tack an Elizabeth death threat onto an existing plot. The opportunity came in 1594. The unfortunate casualty of his scheme was Elizabeth's doctor, Roderigo Lopez (1525–94). Not only was a doctor open to accusations of a poison plot, but Lopez was Jewish by birth. Anti-Semitism was never far below the surface of Elizabethan England.*

* A fact exploited by Shakespeare in his play *The Merchant of Venice*, written just two years after the allegations against Lopez caused a sensation.

Who was Lopez?

- He had fled his birthplace, Portugal, to escape the Portuguese 'Inquisition' and where he'd have been labelled a Marrano (a hidden Jew).
- In England he was seen as a practising Christian and loyal to Elizabeth's Protestant faith.
- He became a popular physician to the influential people in England, treating Elizabeth's favourite, Leicester, and her spy-master, Francis Walsingham.
- A 1584 pamphlet accused Lopez of being in league with Leicester to distil poisons. That mud did not seem to stick at the time. He went on to become physician-in-chief to Queen Elizabeth.
- The queen rewarded him for his services with monopolies on the import of aniseed and sumac that made his fortune.

So by 1594 Lopez was a wealthy and respected senior citizen … despite the lingering racial prejudice. He had only one real enemy. Unfortunately it was Elizabeth's latest 'favourite', the Earl of Essex. It seems Essex had been treated by Lopez and the doctor had broken the patient-confidentiality rules.

> 'I'll be revenged on the whole pack of you.'
>
> *Malvolio,* Twelfth Night, *William Shakespeare*

Essex bided his time till along came the Don Antonio connection. The Don (who was not a Mafioso boss) was a near-derelict pretender to the Portuguese throne. Elizabeth tolerated him around her court thinking he might be a useful pawn in the game against Spain.

Two of the Portuguese Don's servants were arrested for being double-agents in the pay of Spain. It emerged that the suspects had been in correspondence with Dr Lopez. Essex made his move and had Dr Lopez arrested.

His house was searched but nothing incriminating was found. Elizabeth was furious. Her top spy, Walsingham, would know the truth. As a patient of Lopez himself, Walsingham would be sure of the doctor's innocence. Elizabeth raged at Essex, saying he was …

> 'A rash and temerarious youth, to enter into the matter against the poor Doctor Lopez, which he could not prove, but whose innocence she knew well enough.'
>
> *Quoted in Lytton Strachey's* Elizabeth and Essex *(1928)*

Essex did what any young hothead would do. He sulked for two days. Then he began to plot a furious revenge. Portuguese messengers were intercepted and with a little persuasion from racks and red-hot pincers they implicated Dr Lopez. Elizabeth was inclined to release the Jewish doc, but one witness made an unequivocal claim: Lopez had agreed to poison the queen on behalf of Spain, for a price of 50,000 crowns.

Confronted with the charge, Lopez confessed … though he claimed he was only interested in extorting money from the King of Spain. 'I wouldn't really hurt Her Maj, honest guv.' Essex was jubilant. He wrote to a friend …

> 'I have discovered a most dangerous and desperate treason. The point of conspiracy was Her Majesty's death. The executioner was to have been Dr Lopez; the manner poison. This I have so followed as I will make it appear clear as noon-day.'

At his trial, Dr Lopez said his confession had been obtained under torture. Today, in most legal systems, that would invalidate the confession. But in Tudor times the circumstances of the confession were irrelevant. A confession is a confession is a confession.

He was sentenced to death by hanging, drawing and quartering. For months Elizabeth procrastinated and failed to sign the execution warrant.

Lopez eventually went to his death maintaining his innocence. He was said to have declared before his death that he loved his queen as well as he loved Jesus. The crowd took the remark as deviously ironic and jeered at the mutilated man.

Elizabeth's instincts were probably right. Yet, delay or no delay, she still sent her doctor to a terrifying death.

> 'Politics have no relation to morals.'
>
> *Niccolò Machiavelli (1469–1527), Italian historian, diplomat*

— WALTER, LEAD ME TO THE ALTAR —

> 'O, my America! My new-found land.
> My kingdome, safeliest when with one man man'd,
> My mine of precious stones, My Emperie,
> How blest I am in this discovering thee!'*
>
> *John Donne (1572–1631), English poet*

* This is NOT a paean to the discovery of America as it seems. It is an erotic love poem about the 'discovery' of his girlfriend's body. She is clearly the original 'American dream'.

Essex wasn't the only favourite vying for the ageing queen's patronage. Walter Ralegh was a soldier, sailor and poet. He was from an old West Country family who'd been reduced to impoverished gentry in Elizabeth's time. When he arrived at court he became a natural enemy of Essex.

The facts and the fictions of Ralegh's life are an embodiment of several of the illusions we have about the Elizabethan era.

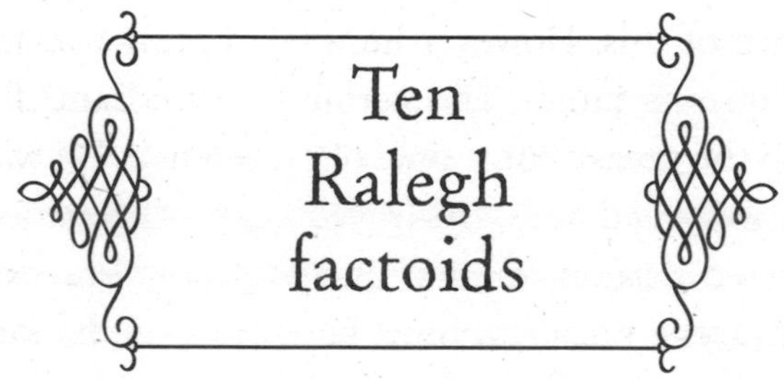

Ten Ralegh factoids

1 Chivalry

Ralegh is most famous for the cloak-and-puddle tale. In the late 1570s Elizabeth looked, dismayed, at a puddle on the path ahead of her. The first recorded version of the story says …

> 'Ralegh cast and spread his new plush cloak on the ground, whereon the queen trod gently. She was grateful for so free and seasonable tender of so fair a foot cloth and bestowed on him many suits.'
>
> *Courtier's description*

This chivalrous act was the making of him. Many historians dismiss the legend as untrue, because it wasn't recorded till 80 years later. But one version of his coat-of-arms features a swirling cloak and seems to suggest the tale is based on fact.

2 Courtly love

> 'I have lived a sinful life, in all sinful callings; for I have been a soldier, a captain, a sea-captain, and a courtier, which are all places of wickedness and vice.'
>
> *Sir Walter Ralegh*

It's a myth that Elizabeth was in love with Ralegh. There is no evidence of this. However he was an attractive man, 20 years the queen's junior, and certainly flirted and flattered his way up the greasy court pole of preference. He was well-educated, well-read and well-travelled, a Renaissance man, who attracted a salon of poets and philosophers, explorers and adventurers. Elizabeth must have enjoyed the kudos he brought to her court. But real passion? No.

3 Patronage

As the old aphorism goes …

> 'It's not *what* you know, it's *who* you know.'*

Elizabeth responded with honours for Ralegh – he was granted the patent for licensing wine sales, a monopoly that brought money and influence. He in turn wrote love poems to his queen. In the overblown poem 'The Ocean To Cynthia',

* In 2014 Lino Carbosiero was made a Member of the Order of the British Empire. What an honour! Did he save lives as a devoted nurse? Did he devote 50 years to helping the homeless or spend 20 years as a school-crossing patrol? No, he was barber to Prime Minister David Cameron. There you have it. A short cut to top honours. It's not what you know … still as true today.

Elizabeth is portrayed as the Goddess of the Moon (which is a bit cheesy). He hailed her as 'the seat of joy's and love's abundance!'

4 Ambition

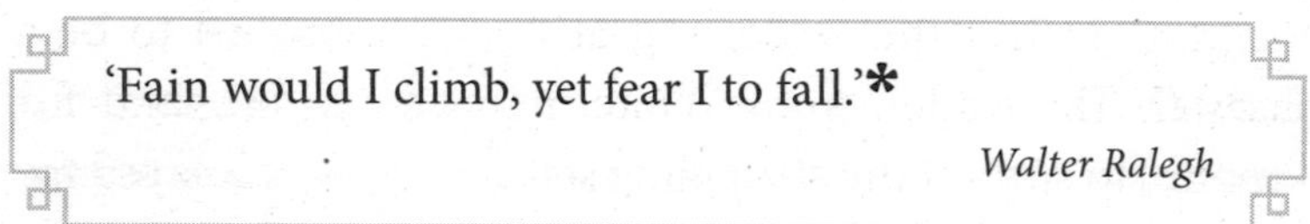

'Fain would I climb, yet fear I to fall.'*

Walter Ralegh

In 1584 Ralegh sponsored England's first voyage to colonize the New World. Ralegh was inspired by the geographer and map-maker Richard Hakluyt (pronounced Hackle-wit) who envisaged overseas colonies in which settlers lived off the land and prospered. Ralegh had a huge hand in creating what is today the USA. In 1587 he became captain of the Queen's Guard, and had the power to develop England's best way of competing with Spain – establishing a colonial empire.

5 Sycophancy

'Knavery and flattery are blood relations.'

Abraham Lincoln (1809–65), US President

It was Sir John Hawkins who'd introduced England to tobacco – thanks Sir John. But it was the showman Ralegh who stole the limelight when he told Elizabeth he could weigh smoke. (He weighed a piece of tobacco, smoked it

---

* According to Thomas Fuller's history, written 60 years later, Ralegh scratched these words on a window pane with a diamond ring. Elizabeth I allegedly scrawled underneath, 'If thy heart fails thee, climb not at all'. Well, it rhymes.

then weighed the ash. The difference was the weight of the smoke.) As an encore, he suggested he name the home of tobacco after her … Virginia.

Elizabeth wouldn't fall for such blatant toadying obsequiousness, would she? She did. She rewarded Ralegh with a knighthood and named him 'Lord and Governor of Virginia'. In fact the settlement at Roanoke proved to be a disaster. The leader, John White, returned to England for supplies to sustain the struggling settlers. He was delayed for three fatal years during which time the Roanoke pioneers disappeared.

Why the delays? First Elizabeth requisitioned White's ships to help in the defence of England against the Spanish Armada … understandable. But when the Spanish had been defeated, and White finally set sail, his crews decided on a little diversion via Cuba to attack Spanish treasure ships – less forgivable. By the time White finally arrived there was no trace of the Roanoke population.*

6 Innovation

> 'Smoking kills. If you're killed, you've lost a very important part of your life.'
>
> *Brooke Shields (1965—), American actress*

The Elizabethan age is remembered as a gateway to the 'modern' world. As the Americas were explored and exploited they became a 'New World' that gifted us new joys like tomatoes, turkeys and potatoes. Such blessings are usually

---

* Top tip here: make your name with a grand idea … then send someone else off to die for it. Ralegh is remembered for his expansionist ideals in North America. It is *forgotten* he never actually *went* to North America.

attended by curses. The curse in this case being tobacco, of course. Ralegh didn't invent smoking but he had a large part in popularising tobacco in court circles.

7 Adventure

> 'He was all the heroes in one magnificent, sexy, animal package. I just wish we had someone around today half as good as Errol Flynn.'
>
> *Jack L. Warner (1892–1978), film studio boss*

Ralegh was the Errol Flynn of his age. A swashbuckling, larger-than-life character and a leader. Ralegh was Captain Blood in the flesh – but without some Hollywood script-writer to give him a happy ending. In 1594 he heard of a 'City of Gold' – El Dorado in the Spanish vernacular – in South America. He sailed off to find it in Venezuela. The trip was not very successful, though to read his exaggerated account you'd think he'd won the lottery, hit the jackpot and seen all his boats come home. He wrote his own Hollywood script in which he was the hero ... others added legends that he was the first European to see the spectacular Angel Falls, when he almost certainly wasn't.* He pursued his El Dorado dream for years until he returned in the mid-1590s. The failure to enrich England would come back to haunt him.

---

* Angel Falls is NOT some romantic Elizabethan naming of a heavenly discovery. It was named after Jimmie Angel, a US pilot, who was the first person to fly over the falls in the 1930s. His ashes were scattered there when he died, which is a bit of a waste. They'll have washed away into the sea by now.

8 Romantic love

> 'Deceiving others. That is what the world calls a romance.'
>
> *Oscar Wilde*

In 1592 Ralegh was 36 when he fell for the 25-year-old Bess Throckmorton. They married in secret. She was pregnant. Shock-horror. They were both in danger if the queen found out, because Elizabeth was guardian to her maidservants and had to give permission before they could marry. The baby was born and Bess tried to return to court as if the marriage and the baby had never happened.* But there was no hope of keeping the secret — not in such a rancorous, back-stabbing court where Ralegh was not everyone's blue-eyed boy. When the queen discovered the truth, she went into a rage. The happy couple were sent to the Tower of London … but Ralegh spent only five weeks there before he was released on probation.

9 Vengeance

To redeem himself, Ralegh was ordered by the queen to carry out 'virtuous' deeds. You know the sort of thing … committing acts of piracy and mass murder on Spanish treasure fleets. His queen and his country needed him. His first task was to avenge the *Revenge* – the ship sunk by the Spanish. He took a squadron to the Azores, where they seized two giant Spanish treasure ships. The queen took

---

* Some reports say the baby was farmed out to a wet nurse and later died of plague. Its life in a noble household like the Raleghs' would probably have been more hygienic and 'safer' for the baby. But 'safety' for Walter and Bess came first. Or is that cynical?

the bulk of the loot — valued at £82,666 (the equivalent of £14 million in today's money).

10 Beheading

> 'The world itself is but a larger prison, out of which some are daily selected for execution.'*
>
> *Sir Walter Ralegh*

Yes, the symbol of the Elizabethan age lost his head … for real, not metaphorically. When the queen died in 1603, Ralegh's fortunes became precarious. James I distrusted Ralegh and that led to a charge that he'd conspired with Spain against James I. It was a stitch-up, but Ralegh was imprisoned in the Tower for most of the rest of his life. He convinced the king to release him for an ill-fated return expedition to Guiana in 1617 in order to obtain the riches he'd failed to find on his first voyage. The expedition was a failure, resulting in the death of his son and the humiliation of his forces. Upon his return he was arrested and informed of his imminent execution. James wanted his new friends, the Spanish, to be appeased. Ralegh was beheaded for treason on 29 October 1618.

Ralegh reportedly said these words on being asked by the executioner which way he wanted to lay his head on the block …

> 'So the heart be right, it is no matter which way the head lies.' *Sir Walter Ralegh, last words*

A heroic character to the very end.

---

* Supposed to have been said by Ralegh to his friends as he was being taken to prison, on the day before his execution.

PURITAN REBELLION: WILLIAM HACKETT 1591

> 'It is a mania shared by philosophers of all ages to deny what exists and to explain what does not exist.'
>
> *Jean-Jacques Rousseau (1712–78), Genevan philosopher*

By the 1590s the Catholics of England were still a real threat to Elizabeth so she was having rebel priests captured and tortured on machines like the rack. You had a choice: you talked or you suffered.

Yet the extreme Protestants, the Puritans, were just as great a menace.

William Hackett was the greatest threat of the 1590s. He had the support of Puritans but, more impressively, he was backed by his dad. And his dad was God … he said.

Words like 'fanatic' and 'deluded' spring to mind these days. But those Elizabethans were superstitious and if someone tells you he's the new Messiah you are not going to call him a liar … just in case he's the real McCoy.

Unlike his predecessor, Jesus, Will Hackett had a temper and a taste for violence. He also seemed to have a taste for human flesh – in one violent alehouse quarrel he bit off the nose of a schoolmaster. Then he had a Damascene conversion and began attracting disciples. When he preached in York and Leicester and Northamptonshire he was usually whipped out of town.

But his attacks on Elizabeth and her government were more serious. He was arrested and bailed. The son of God walked upon England's mountains green and ended up in London around Easter 1591. An MP heard the Hackett rants and said they were a 'wild goose chase with neither head nor foot, rhyme nor reason'.*

His followers began to talk of replacing Queen Elizabeth with King Hackett, and that of course was treason. London was leafleted by the fanatics, Hackett defaced both the royal coat of arms and a portrait of Elizabeth. When arrested, he pleaded guilty to the capital offence of striving to replace Elizabeth – so he'd be hanged, drawn and quartered for that. He pleaded not guilty to defacing Elizabeth's picture. Why bother? Clearly of unsound mind.

As with the execution of Jesus 1,500 years before, Father did not intervene. There are no reports of Hackett being resurrected.

— TORTURING TUDORS —

> 'The coward wretch whose hand and heart
> Can bear to torture aught below,
> Is ever first to quail and start
> From the slightest pain or equal foe.'
>
> *Bertrand Russell (1872–1970), British philosopher*

Torture. Forcing someone to do something on the pain of death … or the pain of a lot more pain, at the very least.

Torture, Bertrand Russell suggests, is the province of the coward. You treat someone badly when they are in your power. You wouldn't dare try it if they were your equal.

The Elizabethans made themselves expert in the arts of

* What sort of goose chase is it if the goose has neither head nor foot? A very short and successful chase. MPs were never noted for talking sense, so what else can we expect?

torture – the 'art' being in the judgement. Enough torture to make the victim comply or talk … but not enough to snuff their candle before they have done what you want.

The Scavenger's Daughter

The Rack is the most famous torture implement, perhaps, but there were others. Take the Scavenger's Daughter, for example.

In 1581 the Catholic rebel Thomas Coteham lived to tell his grim story…

> 'I was arrested on 20 November 1581 and taken to the Tower of London. I was not taken to a torture chamber. The torture instrument was brought to me. It was made up of two halves of an iron hoop, hinged in the middle. My hands were tied behind me and I was placed in one half of the hoop. The other half closed like a door behind me and crushed me so my knees were pressed tight against my chest. This machine is called the Scavenger's Daughter. I was asked to confess that I was a Catholic. I confessed. Then they asked me to confess that I planned to kill Queen Elizabeth. That was not true. My only crime was to come to England and talk to my fellow Catholics. We wanted Elizabeth off the throne – we did not wish for her death. Never end up in the Scavenger's Daughter.'

Thomas Coteham survived the torture … but was found guilty at his trial and executed.

The Rack

> 'And I can well believe that he was racked that number of times, for he lost through it the proper use of his fingers. He was carried back to York, to be executed and while in prison there he had a discussion with some ministers which he wrote out with his own hand. A part of this writing was given to me. These writings however I could scarcely read at all, because the hand of the writer could not form the letters. It seemed more like the first attempts of a child, than the handwriting of a scholar and a gentleman such as he was.'
>
> *Description of the torture of a Catholic priest in the Tower*

The Rack in the Tower of London was a copy of French models. When John Holland, Duke of Exeter, took over as Constable of the Tower in 1447 he had the rack built for prisoners. So the Tower torturers had a pet name for the cruel machine … 'The Duke of Exeter's daughter'.

It was used on prisoners for the next 200 years. It was even used on a woman, Anne Askew, in 1546. As Henry VIII was dying there were struggles to form a council that would control young Edward's kingdom. Anne was a church rebel and the conservatives thought they could get her to betray radical Protestants in court and keep them out of power. She refused to talk and name her fellow radicals. So she was tortured. The only woman ever to be tortured in the Tower of London.

The conservative Lord Chancellor, Richard Rich, and the Earl of Southampton worked the rack themselves – not afraid to get their hands dirty, then.* Anne said …

* Richard Rich was a great survivor. He remained powerful when Mary Tudor came to the throne and went on persecuting Protestants.

> 'Master Rich the torturer put me on the rack till I was nearly dead … When I was set loose I fainted. They woke me up and then put me on the rack again.'

Anne was stretched so much she couldn't walk. She was carried out of the Tower to Smithfield and burned alive, along with two others. A report said …

> 'And thus the good Anne Askew, having passed through so many torments, having now ended the long course of her agonies, being compassed in with flames of fire, as a blessed sacrifice unto God, she slept in the Lord AD 1546, leaving behind her a singular example of Christian constancy for all men to follow.'
>
> *John Foxe* * *(1516–87), English martyrologist:* Acts and Monuments

John Foxe wrote that gunpowder was used to 'rid her of her pain'. But another account said that the execution lasted about an hour and that Anne was most likely unconscious after about 15 minutes. Was the gunpowder ineffective?

Whatever the truth, the spectators were impressed by Anne Askew's bravery, by the fact that she didn't cry out or scream in pain until the flames reached her chest. She died the same way she had lived through her torture, with fortitude.

> 'Rather death than false of faith.'
>
> *Inscription on a portrait of Anne Askew*

---

* Foxe was as responsible as anyone for creating the image of the queen as 'Bloody Mary'. His *Book of Martyrs* became a bestseller, read almost as widely as the Bible. Bloody burnings are bad for bodies but brilliant for business.

The rack master

> 'Torture is such a slippery slope; as soon as you allow a society or any legal system to do that, almost instantly you get a situation where people are being tortured for very trivial reasons.'
>
> *Iain Banks (1954–2013), Scottish author*

By the time Elizabeth came to the throne the top torturer was Richard Topcliffe. He was tailor-made for the job because he was a sadist. He became the queen's pet psychopath who enjoyed torturing on behalf of Elizabeth and her ministers. He boasted that his own instruments and methods were better than the authorized ones, and was allowed to create a torture chamber in his home in London. How did he furnish the rest of the house? Did he have magazine racks? Toast racks? Wine racks?

Topcliffe was described by one of his victims as 'old and hoary and a veteran in evil'.

The Tower of London's 'rack' machine used a system of pulleys and levers to stretch the person until their joints separated. Not only did they separate the joints but the victim's muscles were stretched so far that in most cases they were rendered useless. You can hear the cartilage popping as it snaps when the body has been stretched too far.

While the stretching was going on, the torturers might amuse themselves by burning your ankles and pulling out your toenails. Other prisoners may be invited to watch your suffering as it might encourage them to talk.

The torturer Topcliffe repeatedly raped one of his prisoners, Anne Bellamy, until she betrayed the Catholic priest Robert Southwell. (When Bellamy became pregnant by Topcliffe in 1592, she was forced to marry his servant to cover up the scandal.)

Southwell was duly arrested and handed over to the tender mercies of Topcliffe. But Southwell proved one of the torturer's great failures.

A team of Topcliffe's torturers failed to get the priest to betray his friends. After a month of trying, he was left 'hurt, starving, covered with maggots and lice, to lie in his own filth'.

> 'Stubborn and ardent clinging to one's opinion is the best proof of stupidity.'
>
> *Michel de Montaigne (1533–92), French writer*

The priest was finally hanged, drawn and quartered in 1595 after two and a half years in Topcliffe's prison. He had been a moderate – loyal to the pope AND to the queen.

Southwell's prominent Catholic friends presented Elizabeth with Southwell's testimony and it moved her to display 'signs of grief'. Topcliffe had killed the man who could have helped reach a blood-free compromise. Elizabeth's tears were too little too late to save her country from more years of religious warfare.

> 'I have been tortured ten times. I had rather have endured ten executions. I speak not this for myself, but for others; that they may not be handled so inhumanely, to drive men to desperation, if it were possible.'
>
> *Robert Southwell (1561–95), Catholic priest*

Hanging in chains

A Catholic priest called Father John Gerard survived the torture of Topcliffe and Tower Lieutenant William Waad and lived to tell the tale.

First they tried intimidation. As Gerard explained …

> 'Then they began to entreat me not to force them to do what they were loath to do. Then we proceeded to the place appointed for the torture. We went in a sort of solemn procession, the attendants preceding us with lighted candles, because the place was underground and very dark, especially about the entrance. It was a place of immense extent, and in it were ranged divers sorts of racks, and other instruments.
>
> Some of these they displayed before me, and told me I should have to taste them every one.'

When that didn't work, they resorted to hanging him in chains. Painfully.

> 'Then they led me to a great upright beam or pillar of wood which was one of the supports of this vast crypt. At the summit of this column were fixed certain iron staples for supporting weights.
>
> Here they placed on my wrists gauntlets of iron, and ordered me to mount upon two or three wicker steps; then raising my arms, they inserted an iron bar through the rings of the gauntlets and then through the staples In the pillar, putting a pin through the bar so that it could not slip.'

> 'My arms being thus fixed above my head, they withdrew those wicker steps I spoke of, one by one, from beneath my feet, so that I hung by my hands and arms. The tips of my toes, however, still touched the ground, so they dug away the ground beneath for they could not raise me higher.'

The effect was agony for the priest …

> 'The worst pain was in my breast and belly, my arms and hands. It seemed to me that all the blood in my body rushed up my arms into my hands; and I was under the impression at the time that the blood actually burst forth from my fingers and at the back of my hands. This was, however, a mistake; the sensation was caused by the swelling of the flesh over the iron that bound it.'

They tried the bad-cop/good-cop routine with the jailer being the good guy …

> 'My gaoler also remained, I fully believe out of kindness to me, and kept wiping away with a handkerchief the sweat that ran down from my face the whole time, as indeed it did from my whole body. So far, indeed, he did me a service; but he never stopped entreating and beseeching me to have pity on myself, and tell these gentlemen what they wanted to know.'

When kindness didn't work, they tried horror – three or four men gathered in the chamber and talked aloud: 'He'll be crippled all his life ... if he lives through it. But he'll have to be tortured daily until he confesses.'

Finally they gave him some relief before reapplying the torture ...

> 'I had hung in this way till after one of the clock as I think, when I fainted. How long I was in the faint I know not, perhaps not long; for the men who stood by lifted me up, or replaced those wicker steps under my feet, until I came to myself; and immediately they heard me praying they let me down again. This they did over and over again when the faint came on, eight or nine times before five of the clock.'

In the end it was Waad who cracked ...

> 'Somewhat before five came Waad again, and drawing near, said, "Will you yet obey the commands of the queen and the council?"
>
> "No," said I, "what you ask is unlawful, therefore I will never do it."
>
> Upon this Waad suddenly turned his back in a rage and departed, saying in a loud and angry tone, "Hang there, then, till you rot!"'
>
> Life of Father John Gerard, *autobiography*

Brave Gerard resisted three days of this treatment before he managed to escape with the help of a rope from the Tower.

He died in 1637 at the age of 73 in Rome. Being tortured wasn't always fatal.

Topcliffe died in 1604 at the age of 73. Being a torturer wasn't that bad for the health either.

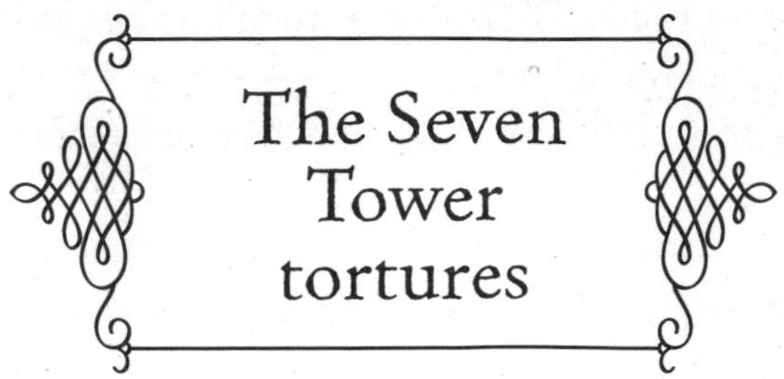

The Seven Tower tortures

An English Catholic prisoner, Edward Rishton, said there were seven tortures to fear in the Tower of London. As well as describing the Rack and the Scavenger's Daughter, he listed …

- 'The Pit – a subterranean cave, 20 feet deep and entirely without light.
- The Little Ease. A dungeon so small as to be incapable of allowing a man to stand erect.
- The iron gauntlet which encloses the hand with the most excruciating pain.
- Chains or manacles attached to the arms.
- Fetters by which the feet are contained.'

Take your pick. Good of Rishton to share that with his fellow Catholics. 'Look at the treats in store if you rebel, my friends.' He probably did a better deterrent job than any government propaganda.

Of course the mental torture of incarceration is the unwritten eighth cruelty … and the diseases you could catch were the ninth.

In 1585 the Catholic-leaning Earl of Arundel was arrested and locked in the Tower, stripped of his wealth and power. After ten years he was suffering from dysentery and felt close to death. He petitioned the queen to be allowed to see his wife and his son, a son he'd never met, one last time before his death.

Elizabeth agreed … on condition he attended a Protestant service in a Protestant chapel. 'If he will but once attend the Protestant Service, he shall not only see his wife and children, but be restored to his honours and estates with every mark of my royal favour.'

Arundel decided he would rather die than comply. He said …

> 'Tell Her Majesty if my religion be the cause for which I suffer, sorry I am that I have but one life to lose.'

He was immediately proclaimed a Catholic martyr. Such a consolation for the son who never had the memory of a meeting with his father to cherish.

Dutch treat

Catholics were tortured and hanged, but never burned. For no logical reason extreme Protestants WERE burned in Elizabeth's reign. In 1575 a twenty-five-strong Anabaptist community was found to be residing in Aldgate, London. Five saw the light of the true Protestant way and recanted* and fifteen were repatriated to Holland. But five intractables were sentenced to be burned alive.

No merciful strangulation for them as they died screaming and roaring, to the horror of witnesses.

---

* If you were horribly cynical you'd say they saw sense – or simply lost their bottle.

Ducking

> 'Sorcerers are too common. There are wizards and white witches in every village which, if they are sought unto, will help almost all infirmities of body and mind …'
>
> *Robert Burton (1577–1640), English scholar:* Anatomy of Melancholy

The ducking stool was a Catch-22 torture. Those accused of witchcraft were strapped to a chair on a beam and lowered into water – a local pond or stream would do. If you floated, the Devil was in you and you were taken out and hanged. If you sank, you probably drowned.

The number of dips depended on the severity of the offence and the cruelty of the mob. A woman could be ducked any number of times, and in some extreme cases the woman would drown.

Ducking was not a Tower torture. It was a speciality for women. In Elizabethan England 90 per cent of those accused of witchcraft were women. (It was a punishment for nagging too.)

– TUDOR THEATRE –

The theatres of Elizabethan England were a novelty but quickly became an institution that was loved or hated by all. The fact that Elizabeth herself was a fan maybe distorts our view of the reality. Some of the characters and their carryings-on tend to be forgotten when we step inside the immaculate reconstruction of the Globe today.

Elizabethan theatres were brilliant and bawdy, creative and cruel, elegant and evil, fantastic and foul … all at the same time.

The businessman: Philip Henslowe (1550–1616)

> 'It is a strange enterprise to make respectable people laugh.'
>
> *Molière (1622–73), French playwright and actor*

A true entrepreneur, Henslowe created theatres in his spare time but made an honest (or dishonest) penny where he could with activities as diverse as money-lending, starch-making and trading in goat skins.

So we shouldn't be surprised that his theatres were multi-purpose too. In 1587 Henslowe built The Rose, the third of the large playhouses in London, which linked seamlessly with his other business – a brothel.*

Did you know … coming up roses

If there is a Rose Alley in your town then it probably has nothing to do with sweet-smelling flowers. In Elizabethan times 'plucking a rose' was a euphemism for having a pee. So Rose Alley would be a popular piddling spot.

In the Paris Garden the main attraction was animal 'baiting', with mastiffs, bears and bulls torn apart for the amusement of the paying public. The plays were a secondary attraction.

> 'Cruelty, like every other vice, requires no motive outside of itself; it only requires opportunity.'
>
> *George Eliot (1819–80), English novelist and journalist*

---

* Henslowe also had a share in the Newington Butts Theatre – and I could not possibly comment on the name. Sometimes a reader must make their own bad jokes.

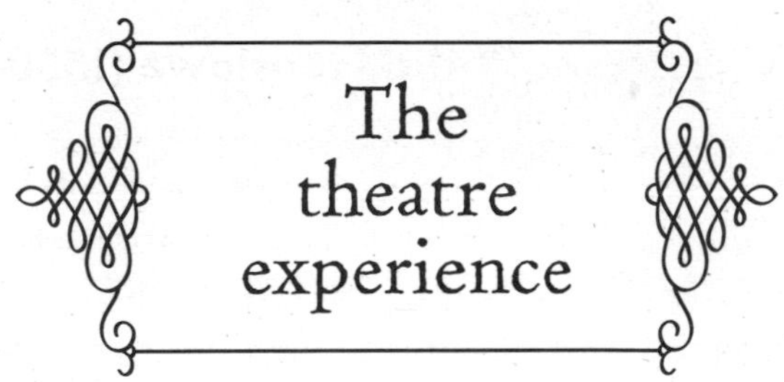

The theatre experience

'We're actors — we're the opposite of people!'

Tom Stoppard (1937–), Czech-born British playwright: Rosencrantz and Guildenstern Are Dead

Nowadays, visiting the theatre seems to be a quiet and respectable pastime. But in Elizabethan times it could be a dangerous day out for Tudors on both sides of the footlights* …

1 Dangerous day for the actors

'But men must know, that in this theatre of man's life it is reserved only for God and angels to be lookers on.'

Francis Bacon (1561–1626),† English statesman, scientist and author

The poorest spectators paid a penny to stand around the stage to watch. Because they stood on the ground they were called 'groundlings'. If they were bored with your performance they

---

* Before writing to complain that footlights hadn't been invented, you can consider 'footlights' a metaphor for the divide between actor and audience. Or you could envision the indoor shows where row of wicks in oil lit the stage … the first footlights.

† A typical Elizabethan polymath with an enquiring mind, Bacon famously died by contracting pneumonia while gathering snow to study the effects of freezing on the preservation of meat. With no one to save his bacon, he'd had his chips.

would simply chat to the people around them and ignore you. If they were really annoyed with your performance then they might decide to throw their fruit or nuts at you.

2 Tudor terror for the spectators (1)

> 'All the world's a stage,
> And all the men and women merely players.'
>
> As You Like It, *William Shakespeare*

All the world becomes a stage when the line between drama and reality becomes blurred. Richer members of the audience would pay two pence to sit in the galleries – rows of seats around three sides of the stage. The richest would pay six pence to sit in 'boxes' – private seats right next to the stage. Some special guests could even sit on the edge of the stage itself. At one performance a spectator on the stage blocked the view of someone in a box. They began to bicker while the actors were trying to perform their play. It ended when the man on the stage drew a sword and stabbed the man in the box … the audience thought this was more fun than the play. (It probably was.)

3 Tudor terror for the spectators (2)

> 'The theatre is certainly a place for learning about the brevity of human glory.'
>
> *Iris Murdoch (1919–99), Irish-born British writer*

Christopher Marlowe had an even more tragic happening at a performance of his *Tamburlaine, Part 2*. In the play the actor portraying the Governor of Babylon is tied to a post and shot. The actor firing the gun aimed to miss, of course. In a November 1587 performance the shot missed the actor by a long way … but killed a woman in the audience.

4 Tudor terror for the theatre owners

> 'O for a Muse of fire, that would ascend
> The brightest heaven of invention,
> A kingdom for a stage, princes to act
> And monarchs to behold the swelling scene!'
>
> Henry V *Prologue, William Shakespeare*

The muse of fire, in a wooden theatre, was unwelcome. In 1613, during a performance of Shakespeare's play *Henry VIII*, a real cannon was used to fire blank shots. The blanks contained cloth wadding, which was meant to end up in the Thames. Unfortunately it drifted onto the thatched roof of the Globe Theatre. The building burned to the ground. When it was rebuilt, the theatre company (sensibly) had the roof covered in tiles.

5 Tudor terror for the theatre companies (1)

Plays were not very popular with the people who ruled the city. A Puritan preacher once said …

> 'Sin causes the plague and plays cause sin. So plays cause the plague.'

Today's equivalent to the Puritans are those who say …

> 'Television can teach your child about violence and aggressive behaviour.'
>
> *Centre for Media Literacy, US agency*

Tudor city councillors complained that the plays drew crowds and caused all sorts of problems like …

- spreading the plague
- fighting and street disturbances
- keeping people from going to church
- robberies
- accidents with collapsing stages

Spreading plague is an accusation that could be levelled against church-going too. Services in Tudor times were not the sanctimonious and tranquil affairs we may imagine. There were frequent complaints about bad behaviour in the pews: talking, eating, spitting, sleeping and pissing during services – with women as guilty as men.

As for the fighting and disturbances in church, it was often the women who were guilty of brawling among themselves. The seating in churches was hierarchical; if a woman lost her high-ranking seat, and felt her status was being usurped by another woman, then a fight might ensue. Pew priority mattered.

6 Tudor terror for the theatre companies (2)

> 'I love the stage, I love the process of acting in theatre, but unfortunately, it doesn't pay the bills.'
>
> *Kabir Bedi (1946—), Indian actor*

Tudor theatre companies had to have a respectable sponsor, otherwise they could be arrested for being tramps and worthless beggars. When the theatres were closed (after accidents or during an outbreak of plague) the actors struggled to make a living. They could go on tour, but touring cost money so their wages would be cut to half. Even the Earl of Pembroke's company struggled during the plague year of 1593. They were forced to sell their costumes and their play books so they could eat. It's easy to see how out-of-work actors could turn into 'rogues, vagabonds and sturdy beggars', and why the law treated them with suspicion.

7 Tudor terror for the theatre companies (3)

> 'Fraud, robbery and murder have characterized the English usurpation of the government of our country. Why, for the last fifty years we have been robbed in the matter of taxes of hundreds of millions.'
>
> *John Edward Redmond (1856–1918), Irish politician*

Theatre companies on tour would do anything for money, and they often gave private performances. When a wealthy man called Gamaliel Ratsey offered a travelling company 40 shillings to perform for him, the actors were thrilled – their most successful shows usually earned them just 20 shillings. They performed, as promised, and Ratsey paid them. The next morning they set off happily for the next town on their tour, but they were stopped in a nearby forest. A highwayman held them at gunpoint. 'You are nothing but a band of thieves,' he told the actors. 'Now, pay me the 40 shillings you stole from Ratsey.' The miserable actors handed the money over. How did the highwayman know about their performance the night before? Because the highwayman was none other than Ratsey himself. (The actors probably had the last laugh. This story was published when Ratsey was hanged for his thieving ways.)

8 Tudor terror for the theatre writers (1)

> 'The first thing we do, let's kill all the lawyers.'
>
> King Henry VI, Part 2, *William Shakespeare*

Playwrights mixed with some fairly rough people. Some of their acting spaces would be used for plays one day and bear-baiting or prize-fighting the next. Shakespeare made clever use of this. In his play *The Winter's Tale*, he brought one of the tame bears on stage to chase a character off. But the violent friends of theatre people could cause more problems. Playwright Ben Jonson was a spy, like Marlowe, and had a part in the arrest of Guy Fawkes in 1605. Jonson killed a man in a sword fight but was set free by the courts.

9 Tudor terror for the theatre writers (2)

> 'I've got a great ambition to die of exhaustion rather than boredom.'
>
> *Thomas Carlyle (1795–1881), Scottish philosopher*

Playwrights made very little money from their plays. They were paid just once for the script. The theatre companies could then perform it as many times as they liked and make a lot of money from it, but the writer never got another penny. The result was playwrights had to find another job – as Shakespeare and Marlowe did – or write an awful lot of plays to make a living. Shakespeare made his money from acting or owning theatres, so he made do with writing a couple of plays each year. Thomas Heywood worked for the Queen's Players from 1605 to 1619 and claimed to have written 220 plays. That's a play every three weeks. Many

Tudor playwrights died at an early age – if a knife didn't kill them then exhaustion did.

10 Tudor terror for the theatre writers (3)

'Who steals my purse steals trash; 'tis something, nothing;
But he that filches from me my good name
Robs me of that which not enriches him,
And makes me poor indeed.'*

Othello, *William Shakespeare*

Writing plays could be a dangerous business! Marlowe, Shakespeare, Kyd and Jonson all spent time in prison for writing plays that annoyed the people in authority.

Plays can carry ideas and if the ideas upset the queen then the playwright would be blamed. The Earl of Essex and his friends plotted to overthrow Elizabeth I. They hired Shakespeare's company to perform *Richard II* – a play about a monarch being overthrown. Elizabeth was furious, Shakespeare was arrested and lucky not to lose his head.

Did you know ... Elizabeth the luvvie

Elizabeth is remembered as a Shakespeare fan. Yet, oddly, she never visited the Bard's Globe Theatre to see a play. She DID however, go there to see bear-baiting. In 1559 she entertained the French ambassador at a

---

* What a noble sentiment. Sadly it was spoken by Iago, one of the greatest villains ever to grace the stages of the world. So we can be very sceptical about believing a villain's opinion. A true hero, like comedian Tony Hancock, would be more likely to say, 'Who steals my purse gets a punch up the bracket.'

baiting in the Paris Gardens. She enjoyed it so much she returned the next day. A potentially dangerous entertainment for Her Majesty; tormented bears had been known to break free and kill spectators. And who can blame the creatures? Chained and plagued by snapping mastiffs, or blinded and stung with whips.

The queen's enjoyment of this cruelty is perhaps an insight into Elizabeth's character. Her actions rather contradict her words, for in a poem bidding au revoir to her last realistic suitor, the Duke of Anjou, she wrote …

'For I am soft and made of melting snow.'

Seems she was not as slushy as all that.

It's certainly a sign of how her world is distant from ours. Philip Stubbes was a rare cry of reason in the slaughterhouse when he wrote, 'What Christian heart can take pleasure to see one poor beast tear, rend and kill another, and all for his foolish pleasure?' Indeed.

– BLOOD SPORT –

William Shakespeare lived in a cruel world. The theatre may seem a gentle entertainment to us today, but in Shakespeare's time theatre buildings were used for some fairly cruel sports when they weren't being used for plays.* A foreign visitor to the Beargarden Theatre in 1584 wrote the following:

> 'There is a round building three stories high in which are kept about a hundred large English dogs, with

* Bear-baiting and bull-baiting took place just once or twice a week. The kind owners decided the tormented animals needed a rest.

> separate wooden kennels for each for them. These dogs were made to fight one at a time with three bears, the second bear being larger than the first and the third larger than the second. After this a horse was brought in and chased by the dogs and, at the end, a bull who defended himself bravely. Next a man threw some white bread among the crowd who scrambled for it. Right over the middle of the place a rose was fixed. This rose was set on fire by a rocket. Suddenly lots of apples and pears fell down upon the people standing below. While people were scrambling for the fruit some rockets were made to fall down on them from above. This caused great fright but amused the spectators. After this rockets and other fireworks came flying out of all corners and that was the end of the entertainment.'

Not everyone enjoyed the theatre or the crowds it attracted. The Puritans objected to theatres whenever they had the chance. In 1596 James Burbage converted some old monastery buildings into an indoor theatre. The district council of Blackfriars was run mainly by Puritans. They were furious and wrote this letter to the government ministers …

> 'James Burbage has bought certain rooms at Blackfriars and means to turn them into a common playhouse. It will grow to be a very great annoyance to the inhabitants of Blackfriars. It will gather together all sorts of vagrant and wicked persons. They will come, pretending to see the plays, but working at all manner of mischief. Also there will be crowds of people cluttering our streets which would be dangerous if God sends us a plague. Besides, this

> playhouse is so near to the church that the noise of drums and trumpets will greatly disturb the preachers and the congregation when they are trying to pray.'

Who do you think won in the case of Burbage? The Puritans, of course.* Burbage was denied permission to put on plays at the theatre. A company of school boys (the Children of the Chapel Royal) were, however, allowed to perform there. In 1606 Shakespeare's company, The King's Men, were finally allowed to put on adult performances there – and the Blackfriars Theatre made him more money than his other London theatres.

* They could have argued that using a monastery site would revive bad habits?

SPY AND EYE

> 'In the tear-filled tide of time,
> Even the oak tree dies.'
>
> *Teresa Williams (1968—), 'Poems'*

The century turned, as centuries tend to do. By 1600 England was stagnating. It was waiting for Elizabeth to die and a new, younger monarch to inject some energy into the country.

BRIEF TIMELINE – FIN DE SIÈCLE

1600 Essex fails to defeat the Irish rebels and his punishment is to have his sweet wine monopoly cut off. He is left relatively impoverished. But …

1601 … then Elizabeth cuts off his head, which leaves him relatively dead. He had tried to lead a popular revolution but the people of England said, 'No thanks,' and left him looking foolish – and headless.

1603 Elizabeth dies. The end of the Tudors, but not the end of Tudor terror and torture. The English throne is taken by the son of Mary, Queen of Scots, James VI of Scotland and I of England. He'd curried favour in England by hinting he'd be tolerant of Catholics. But he isn't, so …

1605 … disappointed Catholics plot to blow James up as he opens Parliament. The gunpowder plot fails and the plotters, including Guy Fawkes, are tortured and executed with torturing Tudor skill. *Plus ça change*.

1616 William Shakespeare dies in retirement – on his birthday – in his Stratford home and may have been forgotten by everyone but …

1623 … Shakespeare's friends publish his plays in book form. The publisher says that the great plays are not for the Tudor age but 'for all time'. We'll never know how great Marlowe's plays could have been because he died so young. The victim of a time-trail of terror that started with Henry VIII …

— THE KIT CONSPIRACY —

> 'You must be proud, bold, pleasant, resolute,
> And now and then stab, when occasion serves.'
>
> *Christopher Marlowe (1564–93), English playwright*

Elizabeth stayed in power by engaging a network of spies. It was a dangerous game and some, like playwright Christopher Marlowe, died playing it. In 1593 the playwright and spy was stabbed through the eye … or was he?

Kit Marlowe was a genius … and three little pigs short of a fairy tale. He led a rebellious and reckless life. He won a place at Cambridge because he was clever, not because he was rich. His father was an artisan (like Will Shakespeare's father), a shoemaker with a large family.

His plays are great work for such a young man. If he had lived to William Shakespeare's age he would surely have been a greater writer. However, his plays did not make him very much money and Kit Marlowe seemed to enjoy making money. He became a spy when still at college. Records of his fights in public show he was hot-tempered and fearless.

Kit died when he was stabbed through the eye in a brawl. The coroner recorded that Marlowe had spent all day in a house in Deptford with three men: Ingram Frizer, Nicholas Skeres and Robert Poley. All three had been employed by one or other of Elizabeth's spy-masters.

> 'Money can't buy love, but it improves your bargaining position.'
>
> *Christopher Marlowe*

Witnesses said that Frizer and Marlowe had argued over the bill (now famously known as 'the Reckoning'). Marlowe snatched Frizer's dagger and wounded him on the head. Frizer struggled and Marlowe was stabbed above the right eye, killing him instantly. The jury concluded that Frizer acted in self-defence, and within a month he was pardoned by Elizabeth.

Others believe Marlowe was lured to the house and murdered. Kit Marlowe found himself in several tricky situations that we know of and escaped them all. Would he have been careless enough to be trapped by enemies and murdered? Or could he have faked his own death to escape his latest troubles?

> 'Our swords shall play the orators for us.'
>
> *Christopher Marlowe*

Marlowe's three dinner companions had shady records, so any statement from them can be treated with suspicion. In addition to being spies, Frizer and Skeres bought and sold property at a profit and they were dishonest money-lenders to innocent victims.

Skeres was almost certainly part of the Babington Plot (see pp. 157–59). He was named (two years after Marlowe's death) as …

> 'One of a number of masterless men and cutpurses, whose practice it is to rob gentlemen's chambers and shops, in and about London.'

Robert Poley was a very experienced spy for Elizabeth. He'd worked as a secret agent for at least 20 years. He was a suspected (but not proven) poisoner. He was credited with tricking Antony Babington into betraying himself.

Babington's last letter to Poley said …

> 'Farewell. You are Sweet Robert (if you have been true to me) or the most evil creature on Earth (if you have not been true to me).'

Poley had not been true, so 'most evil creature' is the more apt description. Poley was so crooked that even his own masters didn't trust him. He even boasted about being a liar, saying …

> 'I will swear to anything so long as it gets me out of trouble.'

If these three swore Marlowe died in an argument, we have very little reason to believe such professional liars.

It's a history mystery with a dozen theories. They include …

- It really WAS an accident but the quarrel was about some cash Marlowe owed to the money-lenders Frizer and Skeres.*
- Marlowe had incriminating evidence against Sir Walter Ralegh, so Ralegh paid the agents to murder him.
- Marlowe was a favourite of spy-master Walsingham, so Walsingham's wife was jealous and SHE had Marlowe murdered.
- His plays were subtle Catholic propaganda so the queen's minister Lord Burghley had Marlowe assassinated.

And most sensational of all the conspiracy theories?

- Queen Elizabeth herself had Marlowe killed because he was an atheist.†

Was the queen the silhouette behind the screen of shadowy dealings?

All we can say for certain is that it was a dangerous life being a spy in Elizabeth's pay.

> 'What are kings, when regiment is gone, but perfect shadows in a sunshine day?'
>
> *Christopher Marlowe*

---

* As if payday loans didn't have a bad enough press, we now discover they've always been ruthless.

† As daft as the theory that Elizabeth wrote Shakespeare's plays … or that Marlowe wrote Shakespeare's plays. Maybe they wrote them together? A great new theory I'm sure someone could 'prove'.

So how did Marlowe die if it's true a dagger entered his eye?

DANGEROUS DAYS DEATH VIII

STABBED THROUGH THE EYE

A flash of silver is all you notice as the point of the blade enters your eye. The initial pain is searing as the front of the eye (cornea) is pierced and the blade goes on, into and through the lens. Momentarily, vision is blurred, before being replaced by a cascade of colour and flashing lights as the knife passes through the liquid jelly of the vitreous humor. As the jelly squelches out down your face, this is the last light you see, for the blade continues on through the bone at the back of the eye (orbit), plunging into your brain.

Hopefully it is a large knife that reaches deep into the brain and fatally damages the areas controlling the heart and breathing, killing you immediately. A headache to die for, some would say!

Dr Peter Fox

— THE MONOPOLY GAME —

'Flattery is all right so long as you don't inhale.'

Adlai E. Stevenson III (1930—), US politician

Granting monopolies made many men rich – as we've seen, Doctor Lopez had the right to impose duties on some spices, Elizabeth's groom-porter licensed gaming houses and the right to supply playing cards and dice, Ralegh held a wine monopoly … Parliament and the people were angry that these monopolies inflated prices. When salt prices doubled in 1601, they protested to the queen.

It gave Elizabeth one of her finest moments since the Armada. In a clever speech she assured her MPs that she was no 'greedy grasping scraper' and would not tolerate monopolies that became 'grievous to my people'. She turned it around. She *agreed* with Parliament. Then she concluded with such a humble, grovelling assurance it is hard to believe Parliament swallowed it. She said …

> 'To be a king and wear a crown is more glorious to them that see it than it is to them that bear it.'

Poor queen … she suffers more than her people. Really?

She could have been echoing her pet poet, William Shakespeare when his Richard II said …

> 'Uneasy lies the head that wears a crown.'

It's interesting that Elizabeth isn't talking only of past monarchs but of future ones – the ones England 'shall have' after she's gone. She is predicting her own demise.

That was odd for Elizabeth. She had steadfastly refused to name an heir. Everyone guessed it would be James VI of Scotland … the son of Mary, Queen of Scots.* Elizabeth refused to confirm it. She thought that as soon as she announced it she'd be deserted by the boot-licking minions

---

* He didn't seem to hold a grudge over the small matter of Elizabeth having his mum's head hacked off. So long as he could get his butt on the English throne, he'd forgive anything.

and the toady yes-men who would be jockeying for a ride on the new young horse. When Parliament demanded she name a successor, she snapped …

> 'Do you think I could love my own winding sheet?'

Elizabeth had her faults, but she understood human nature and the shallow loyalty of the fickle flatterers.

> 'Everyone likes flattery; and when you come to Royalty you should lay it on with a trowel.'
>
> *Benjamin Disraeli (1804–81), British Prime Minister and novelist*

And Elizabeth was right about her own failing body. The end *was* nigh. She was only 67 years old, but the clock was ticking faster.

– THE FINAL PLOT –

> 'Even my close friend in whom I trusted, who ate my bread, has lifted his heel against me.'
>
> *Psalm 41:9*

By the end of the 1500s Elizabeth was ailing. The lead she used in her make-up may have covered her imperfect skin but it weakened her constitution. (No, not the constitution of the English state. It's never had a written one.) What was that white lead doing to her?

DANGEROUS DAYS DEATH IX

LEAD POISONING

Lead interferes with many chemical processes within the body. The journey to death is a magnificent and multi-symptomatic route.

The more common characteristics are headache, depression, stomach pains, diarrhoea, constipation and painful muscles. Much more interesting are the nerve problems which result in a loss of your sex drive, but with the headaches that's not a bad thing. Then there is the effect on your red cells: making them burst and releasing the red stuff (haemoglobin) into the blood stream. You pass it in your wee, which goes a lovely merlot red, but also clogs up your kidneys, putting you into kidney failure.

Meanwhile the lead is damaging the brain, causing it to swell. Trapped within the skull the brain pressure rises, putting you into a coma. Fits follow, with consequent death.

Dr Peter Fox

As Elizabeth's spring began to wind down there were frustrated young subjects fully wound up to take over. If she wouldn't die, then maybe she could 'retire' and leave government to them?

She had survived the plots of so many enemies and now she faced her greatest threat from a friend – a special friend at that. A 'favourite'. The Earl of Essex was the man to play the part of Judas for a metaphorical 30 pieces of silver and the power to command the English.

The queen called the earl her 'Wild Horse'. She had spent years putting up with Essex and his disobedience, his violence and his moods. He could be charming when he wanted, and the handsome young tearaway knew how to flatter the old queen.

The earl thought the people of England were ready for a new leader and decided he was the man to lead them into a new century and a new age after years of famine in which poor people had died on the streets or fed their children on cats, dogs and nettle roots.

The downfall of the 'most popular man in England' (as he had been called) began in Ireland. The Earl of Tyrone was rebelling against English rule and he had support from Elizabeth's old foes, Scotland and Spain. The Earl of Essex lobbied Elizabeth to let him command an army that would crush the upstart Irish.

He set off with 16,000 troops in March 1599 – it was the largest force ever to enter Ireland. It should have been a formality. In fact, Essex managed the war so badly he ended up making a truce with Tyrone.

Did you know … the Essex tactics

The English under Essex were not very impressive in Irish battles but pretty good at cheating.

Essex used a devious trick on the Irishman Sir Brian O'Neill. He …

- went to dinner with Sir Brian
- took his own bodyguard along
- enjoyed the dinner and waited till Sir Brian and his guards had gone to bed

- massacred all the servants in the house
- arrested the sleepy Sir Brian

Sir Brian O'Neill and his wife were sent off to Dublin to be executed. It might have been effective, but it wasn't cricket.

As a man-manager, Essex was all carrot and no stick. He dished out knighthoods to his officers like a children's party clown scatters boiled sweets. At one time it was reckoned half the knighthoods in England had been conferred by Essex. Elizabeth was not amused and the Irish rebels were scornful. A popular jest among them was …

> 'Essex never drew his sword but to make knights.'

The power to make knights was a touchy subject in Elizabeth's mind. A woman called Mary Cleere from Essex said the queen's knighthoods were invalid because no woman had the power to make knights. A harmless if cranky opinion? Mary Cleere was burned at the stake for expressing her views. Touchy subject or hot topic?

Essex had Elizabeth's express order not to return from Ireland until he had defeated the Irish. He chose to disobey. In September 1599 he set sail and reached London four days later. The queen was surprised when he presented himself in her bedchamber one morning at her palace. But the greater crime was to burst into her bedroom before she was fully dressed or in her wig.

First he suffered house arrest. Then in came the punishment. In 1600 Essex was allowed his freedom, but his main source of income – the sweet wines monopoly – was not renewed.

His situation had become desperate, and he shifted from sorrow and repentance to rage and rebellion.

In early 1601 he began to fortify Essex House, his town mansion on the Strand, and gathered a small army. On 8 February he marched through London with some conspirators (who would later be involved in the 1605 Gunpowder Plot) and entered the city to confront the queen.

Essex rode at the head of a hundred horsemen into the City of London. He found that no one would join him. England's most popular man had suddenly become the Invisible Man.

Elizabeth's chief minister (and Essex's most fierce opponent) Robert Cecil had his lordship declared a traitor. His assault through the streets of London was blocked and Essex retired to his house on the Strand. The house was surrounded and he was forced to surrender.

He probably held out a hope of another pardon from Elizabeth. It wasn't forthcoming.

The Earl of Essex had always been a hot-head. On 25 February 1601 he became a no-head when the executioner's axe fell. Robert Cecil would like to have seen him hanged and gutted like the traitor he was, but the queen spared him that at least.

EPILOGUE

> 'For in that sleep of death what dreams may come,
> When we have shuffled off this mortal coil,
> Must give us pause – there's the respect
> That makes calamity of so long life.'
>
> Hamlet, *William Shakespeare*

As Elizabeth lay dying what dreams visited her fevered mind, what images rose from the candle-shadows to haunt her? The execution of her nearest and dearest … of Mary, Queen of Scots, and Essex? Or Tom Seymour, or the hundreds of Catholics she sent to their too-early graves? Her long-dead mother and sad stepmothers?

Or did she think and fret on her legacy? Would she be revered or reviled as she lay in her grave?

> 'On my tombstone I just want it to say, "I'm Cold".'
>
> *Sarah Silverman (1970—), American comedian*

As she declined, so did England. She left behind a stagnating country, poisoned by festering religious sores as deep and deadly as the abscess on Henry VIII's leg. She left behind a country that struggled to survive on a burgeoning slave trade and a fragile rule of the waves.

She gave her name to an era that is remembered by some historians as a 'Golden Age'.

> 'The long reign of Elizabeth I, 1558–1603, was England's Golden Age. Merry England, in love with life. It expressed itself in music and literature, in architecture and in adventurous seafaring.'
>
> *Encyclopaedia Britannica*

How sweet. But not very balanced.

For the timeless poetry of Shakespeare and Marlowe there was the torturing glee of Waad and Topcliffe.

For the adventurous seafaring success of Drake and Ralegh there were hundreds of forgotten swabbies and leathernecks who died of diseases or drowned in the deep.

It was the age of sophisticated spying that could lead you to painful punishment.

A queen on the throne did nothing for women's rights – they were second-class citizens.*

> 'It is extraordinarily entertaining to watch the historians of the past entangling themselves in what they were pleased to call the "problem" of Queen Elizabeth. They invented the most complicated and

* It was NOT an Elizabethan man who said, 'If there's one thing worse than a male chauvinist pig it's a woman who won't do what she's told' … but it could have been.

> astonishing reasons both for her success as a sovereign and for her tortuous matrimonial policy. She was the tool of Burleigh, she was the tool of Leicester, she was the fool of Essex; she was diseased, she was deformed, she was a man in disguise. She was a mystery, and must have some extraordinary solution. Only recently has it occurred to a few enlightened people that the solution might be quite simple after all. She might be one of the rare people who were born into the right job and put that job first.'
>
> *Dorothy L. Sayers (1893–1957), English crime writer*

How did she survive those dangerous days? The plots and enmities of individuals, cabals and whole nations? The schemes to assassinate her or depose her, invade her land or crush her Church?

Probably because, on balance, she was popular. Her (prejudiced) godson put it succinctly …

> 'We did all love her, for she said she loved us.'
>
> *Sir John Harington*

Isn't that the secret of success in politics? Let the people who keep you in power think that you love them?

She TOLD the people how grateful they were towards her. Always a sound tactic to confound critics …

> 'I do not so much rejoice that God hath made me to be a queen, as to be a queen over so thankful a people.'
>
> *Elizabeth I*

Elizabeth was petulant and cruel, self-serving and self-centred. But she knew how to manipulate the people. Her most famous speeches (even if they are distorted in the telling) are master classes in caring condescension …

> 'Yet although God hath raised me high, yet this I esteem the most glory of my crown, that I have reigned with your loves.'
>
> *Elizabeth I, last speech to Parliament (1601)*

Ah, my people, she was saying, you didn't put me on the throne. God did that. But thanks anyway for supporting me … and God.

She went on to modestly say there may be greater monarchs, but (in boastful contradiction) she is top of the class when it comes to monarchs who love the English people.

> 'Though you have had and may have mightier and wiser princes sitting in this seat, yet you never had nor shall have any that will love you better.'

She doesn't *name* the greater predecessors, of course.*

Elizabeth circumvented the concerns that a woman can't be as great as a man with the simple expedient of saying she WAS a man in all that matters …

> 'I have the heart of a man, not a woman, and I am not afraid of anything.'

Then more contradiction. While declaring her *manly*

---

* Perhaps she could have given a name check to Richard III at that point? After all, *he* loved the country so much he died on the battlefield for it. Why the omission? Ah, yes, because her own grandfather, Henry VII, was the man who usurped Richard III's throne and killed him.

qualities, in the next breath of the same speech she is playing on her *womanly* status.

> 'And I pray you that before these gentlemen depart into their countries, you bring them all to kiss my hand.'

We can be sure Henry VIII didn't suggest that all the MPs line up to kiss him on the hand.

In the end she died a lonely woman. She was not a truly 'old' woman by today's standards – she was just 69 when she hopped the royal twig. A woman who went through life swearing that she loved God yet, at the very end, seemed desperate not to meet him (or her).

She struggled for life. She refused to be put to bed by her doctors. Forty years before she had struggled to stay out of the Tower of London lest she never get out of it again. Now, she struggled to stay out of bed, fearing she'd leave it in a shroud.

When chief minister Robert Cecil told her that she must go to bed, she said to him:

> 'The word MUST is not to be used to princes, little man, little man. Ye know I must die, and that makes ye so presumptuous.'

Servants were instructed to make a bed of cushions on which she reclined, delirious and waving a rusty sword at the assassins of her mind.

She raged against the dying light, crying …

> 'All my possessions for a moment of time.'

She discovered, as the mighty always do, that endless time is not for sale. The deaths of her friends depressed her. She developed a 'settled and unremovable melancholy complaining of many infirmities suddenly to have overtaken her'.

Her coronation ring was one of her most prized possessions. She had never taken it off in all the 44 years of her reign and by the time of her last illness it had grown into her flesh. Her doctors insisted it be cut free. Within a week she was dead.

Elizabeth was probably suffering from pneumonia and her fevered brain seemed to dwell on the regrets of her life. If we can believe reports, it was the subject of Ireland that haunted her rather than the ghosts of Mary, Queen of Scots, or Essex. She allegedly said …

> 'I find that I sent wolves not shepherds to govern Ireland, for they have left me nothing but ashes and carcasses to reign over.'
>
> *Elizabeth I*

She slipped away muttering something. Charles Howard, 1st Earl of Nottingham, said she murmured, 'Our cousin of Scotland.' Howard may have invented that, but no one cared. It was what everyone expected and ensured a smooth succession, despite her previous refusals. She understood human nature.

> 'I do not choose that my grave should be dug while I am still alive.'
>
> *Elizabeth I*

Lady Philadelphia Scrope was present. She was a cousin to Queen Elizabeth – her grandmother was the sister of Anne Boleyn. She took the ring that had been cut from Elizabeth's finger – the ruby, mother-of-pearl and diamond ring that bore enamelled portraits of Queen Elizabeth and her mother, Anne Boleyn.

The ring was a valuable work of art. But as a symbol, to Elizabeth, it was priceless. It was her coronation ring and she had held it aloft, declaring …

> 'Behold the pledge of this, my wedlock and marriage with my kingdom. And do not upbraid me with miserable lack of children: for every one of you, and as many as are Englishmen, are children and kinsmen to me.'*

If Elizabeth had been wedded to England, then Lady Scrope's removal of the ring was the decree nisi.

She passed the ring through the window to her brother, Sir Robert Carey. This clever and energetic man had done a good job in keeping law and order on the border with Scotland but now was at Richmond Palace with a relay of horses waiting. He was liked by James VI of Scotland and often carried messages from Elizabeth.

As soon as he received the ring, Sir Robert set off. He galloped past the carts full of plague corpses in the narrow London streets. He rode across the defensive ditches surrounding the capital – ditches dug to defend the city

* This 'marriage' to her kingdom is a defining symbol of her reign. Yet her sister Mary had already used that bit of blarney to sweet-talk the English people. When Mary's marriage to Philip was decried as selling the kingdom to Spain, Mary defended herself by proclaiming she was married to the realm first. Sound familiar?

against an expected invasion from Scotland. It was to be a peaceful invasion when it came.*

Carey made an awesome ride from London to Edinburgh in 60 hours to be first to James with the news.†

The news was simple. When Elizabeth died, the Tudor era was at an end. The dangerous days of Elizabeth I were over. Of course, history being what it is, the new Stuart age would merely offer *newer* dangers, not *fewer* dangers. Dangers like the king and his lords being blown into the skies of London as he opened Parliament. Dangers like his son Charles losing his head to the axeman and the country descending into Civil War.

The English people rejoiced at the dawning of the new age and were blessed, as we all are, by being unable to see into the future.

We *can* look back. Hindsight is 20–20 and we can see that Elizabeth had presided over a brutal age. We can see that now. But should we care? For, as a worldly-wise woman once said …

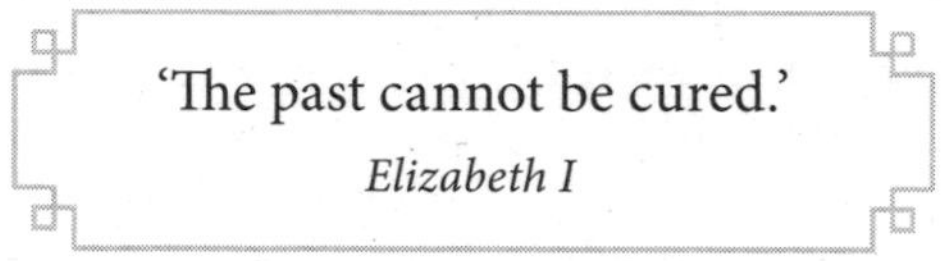

'The past cannot be cured.'

Elizabeth I

The End

---

* Delayed by a year so, James could be sure the plague had disappeared from the capital of his new kingdom. 'Diffidence is the mother o' safety', as they say in Scotland. But his advisers should have told him, 'Ye are feart for the day ye niver seen.'

† Carey hoped this would earn him a good reward. It was a long time before this chancer was given it. Today he'd be an ambulance-chasing lawyer.

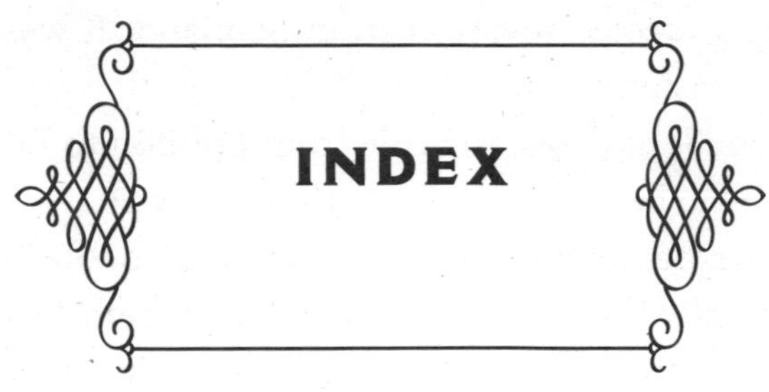

INDEX